THE POWER OF
ACCEPTANCE

FINDING PEACE FROM ANXIETY AND PANIC ATTACKS

JUDITH BEMIS

PUBLISHED BY COLD TREE PRESS
NASHVILLE, TENNESSEE

Published by Cold Tree Press, Nashville, Tennessee

For information regarding permission, write to:
Cold Tree Press, 214 Overlook Court, Suite 253, Brentwood, Tennessee 37027.

Library of Congress Control Number: 2008931611

ISBN-13: 978-1-58385-277-4
ISBN-10: 1-58385-277-8

In loving memory of my husband,
Alpheus Cutler Bemis

One school is finished,
and the time has come for another to begin.

"I'm ready," he said at last.
And Jonathan Livingston Seagull rose with the two starbright gulls
to disappear into a perfect dark sky.

Richard Bach, *Jonathan Livingston Seagull*

CONTENTS

FOREWORD

By Daniel J. Reidenberg, Psy.D., FAPA

Executive Director, SAVE

Fellow and Diplomate, American Psychotherapy Association

W hat led you to pick up this book? Was it the title, the rays of sun on the cover? Maybe it was the word *power,* or the word *acceptance.* Possibly it was the hope you felt when you read that there could be peace from anxiety and panic attacks.

Anxiety disorders frighten, humiliate, and disable over 30 million people. The most common psychiatric illness in America today is anxiety. It affects people of all ages and colors, of all religious and ethnic backgrounds. It scars individuals and families with lost relationships, lost jobs, and financial burdens. It causes anger, frustration and turmoil.

If you are one of those 30 million, you know what it's like to have a pounding, racing heart, sweaty palms—and symptoms that go on forever. You know what it's like when you can't think straight, when panic leaps up without reason or warning, and you feel like you're losing your mind. You know what it's like to go to the hospital, afraid you are dying.

Good news! *The Power of Acceptance* can help you recover from anxiety and panic. Twenty years ago you couldn't go into a bookstore and find many self-help books on this topic. Books that would help you understand how and why acceptance heals.

Judy Bemis is seen by many as a self-help pioneer in making sense of this disorder. She has tried the treatments, done the research, and read the books. She has created a support group and a recovery program.

Now, she has written this book for you. Judy takes you on a journey of soul-searching discovery, and does not shy away from discussing the challenges and setbacks that could have kept her from living life fully. She shares her personal story, and those of others, to help you relate, understand, and connect with her as you walk your path to recovery.

Written with frankness and sincerity, she explains the origins of anxiety and panic, and then breaks new ground by revealing the power of acceptance. It is acceptance, paradoxically, that allows for peace and healing. She explains how *acceptance does not mean giving in.*

Reading this book, you can learn to accept the anxiety and panic rather than fight it. You can learn that although anxiety and panic happen, you can still be okay. (It's just who you are, sometimes for a moment, sometimes for a day.) You are encouraged to accept your feelings, take charge of your life, and become comfortable in your own skin. Concepts unfamiliar to anxiety and panic sufferers.

Complementing the personal stories of Bemis and members of her support group, you will find discussions about self-esteem, good boundaries, family dynamics; you will learn about lowering expectations, eliminating time limits, and allowing for setbacks. What

Bemis has captured on the following pages is the key to success from a true, survivor perspective.

As you sit down with *The Power of Acceptance,* take a deep breath. Be present—right here, right now. As you begin reading, allow a calm, centered feeling to arise. Be open to the idea that acceptance can break the anxiety–panic cycle and that you can experience a freedom you never thought possible.

PREFACE

During the summer of 1965 I would have given anything to have had the information on anxiety disorders that is available today. Alone with my ever-increasing anxiety and panic symptoms, and unaware of what was happening to me, I retreated into a world surrounded by an invisible wall. I was terrified to leave my apartment, to drive, shop, or go to restaurants. My life was ruled by fear. Yet over time, I learned to create a "safe" environment, stay within its perimeters, and when necessary, white-knuckle my way through uncomfortable situations.

A severe setback in 1981 prompted me to once again seek the help of a professional therapist. My panic attacks were out of control and I found myself in an all too familiar pattern of avoidance. Through cognitive-behavioral therapy, I learned the necessary skills that would eventually lead to my recovery. I was faced with many challenges, but throughout those twelve months of therapy, I never gave up. During this time, I found it necessary to change some of my beliefs about personal expectations, dealing with troublesome thoughts, and being in control. I learned important coping strategies and a new way of talking to myself. It was this new self-talk that was crucial to my recovery.

Having moved beyond my own fear, I felt as though I had a mission. With anxiety and panic no longer ruling my life, I wanted to share my newfound freedom with others so that they too could live anxiety and panic-free. The question was, How could I reach other people with this problem? When a friend of mine suggested forming a support group, I was hesitant. How could I do this? I had no credentials. I quickly reminded myself that I had all the credentials I needed: eighteen years of my own prison walls *and the key that unlocked the door.* This was the beginning of Open Door, a network of support groups for persons with agoraphobia and other anxiety disorders.

Once the support groups were established, a program was developed to provide structure to our meetings. Along with group members, and later with therapist Amr Barrada, a list of strategies was then drawn up. The list eventually led to a book entitled, *Embracing the Fear: Learning to Manage Anxiety and Panic Attacks.* When it was published in 1994, I had no immediate plans for writing another book on anxiety disorders. It wasn't until I received a letter from a reader—"I'm looking forward to your next book"—that I seriously considered the idea.

It is always gratifying to receive letters from readers who say the book had a great impact on their lives and gave them hope for recovery. One woman wrote that after twenty-five years of agoraphobia *Embracing the Fear* gave her a program that was helpful; and another stated that her recovery began with reading *Embracing the Fear.*

What made this program so meaningful to them? In a word, compassion. Compassion comes from being there. It comes from knowing what it's like to experience uncontrollable waves of panic, or to experience intense anxiety that just doesn't let up. It comes from having to make up constant excuses for why we can't go to the mall, the corner grocery store, or why it is we can't drive on the highway or ride as a passenger in a car the way everyone else does. It comes from watching our life pass us by, wondering if we will ever be part of it again. Compassion also comes from working with the many anxiety and panic sufferers who have attended the Open Door support groups over the years, and hearing their stories. It comes from seeing their frustration as they try to understand and accept the unpredictability of their anxiety or panic attacks and their recurring setbacks.

Dr. Claire Weekes refers to this problem as an illness of repetition.[1] There is constant repetition of our panic attacks, anxiety, and setbacks. They occur over and over again. Trying hard to be accepting of our situation, we repeatedly pick ourselves up and start over, discouraged, frustrated and frightened. But we do pick ourselves up each time and go on. This takes a great deal of inner strength and courage on our part and we need to remind ourselves of that. In spite of our struggle with anxiety and panic attacks, we truly are survivors. Through the Power of Acceptance, may you come to

---

1 Weekes, Claire. *Simple, Effective Treatment of Agoraphobia*. New York: Bantam Books, 1976. pages 109-110.

understand its meaning, realize its power, and see how it plays an important part in your recovery. May you find comfort in knowing that you are not alone.

I am a teacher by profession, not a therapist. Most of the information in this book is based on my own personal experience and that of members of the Open Door support groups. I have researched all the facts concerning anxiety disorders and have carefully footnoted my findings. The suggestions in this book do not take the place of the advice or care given by a professional therapist or physician.

ACKNOWLEDGMENTS

I want to thank Daniel Reidenberg, Psy.D., FAPA, Executive Director of SAVE, who reviewed the first draft of this book, followed its development, and offered invaluable help with both content and format. His enthusiasm gave me the encouragement and ongoing support I needed to complete this important project. I would also like to thank Amr Barrada, Ph.D., therapist and co-author of *Embracing the Fear: Learning to Manage Anxiety and Panic Attacks*. His review of the second draft led to further insights on its concepts. It was Amr Barrada who first introduced me to a self-talk based on acceptance. For this, I am deeply grateful. I sincerely appreciate the generous time allotted by these two therapists, and value their professional advice.

I will always be grateful for the loving support and encouragement of my late husband, Al Bemis. He was my strongest advocate and a proud supporter of my work for Open Door. His knowledge of the computer was everso helpful in the preparation of the manuscript. He would be pleased to know that it is now in book form.

Many thanks to my editor, Tim McIndoo, who worked on the final editing of *The Power of Acceptance*. His meticulous detail and valuable insight helped shape this book into its final form. I appreciate his skill and sensitivity in preparing this book for publication. Tim was editor for *Embracing the Fear*. It was a pleasure working with him again.

I feel fortunate to have had the opportunity to work with Peter Honsberger and his staff at Cold Tree Press. I had complete confidence that their professionalism and commitment to quality would produce a book of high standards. I especially want to thank Amanda Butler for creating an interior design and cover that truly reflect those standards.

I want to express my appreciation to Open Door members and associates who shared their personal stories in the following pages. Their courage and perseverance will serve as an inspiration to our readers. The anxiety management strategies in chapter 2 were discussed at Open Door meetings. The important feedback from group members helped clarify the information that would be useful to readers.

A number of authors have written on the subject of anxiety disorders, and some of them are quoted in the following pages, especially Edmund J. Bourne, Denise Beckfield, Reneau Z. Peurifoy, and the late Dr. Claire Weekes. Their writing has been an inspiration and an important part of my research. I admire their dedication to helping people recover from anxiety and panic disorders.

In 2007, Open Door merged with NAMI Minnesota (National Alliance on Mental Illness). I am grateful to Sue Abderholden,

Executive Director of NAMI Minnesota, and Ron Reed, former President and CEO of St. Paul Family Service, who made this merger possible. Because of their efforts, Open Door is now more visible to the public, offering hope and support to the many people who try to cope with anxiety and panic attacks in their daily lives.

INTRODUCTION

*T*he *Power of Acceptance* is written for those who suffer from generalized anxiety, panic attacks, agoraphobia and other anxiety disorders. Its purpose is threefold: to gain a better understanding of anxiety disorders in general; to offer coping strategies based on acceptance; and to offer reassurance that there is hope for recovery.

For readers familiar with *Embracing the Fear: Learning to Manage Anxiety and Panic Attacks* (Hazelden Publishing, 1994), the anxiety management concepts in this book will sound familiar. Many of the same coping strategies are used but new insights are offered. For readers unfamiliar with *Embracing the Fear*, the coping strategies will most likely come as a surprise: they are not necessarily based on logic and many are built on paradox. For example, you may find it difficult to believe that you can alleviate your symptoms by letting them be rather than trying to control them. You might wonder how giving yourself permission to leave an uncomfortable situation can actually make it easier for you to stay. And you might wonder how lowering your expectations can help you to approach feared situations with less anxiety. But it was by using these paradoxes (not to be confused with "paradoxical therapy") that I found recovery.

The Power of Acceptance continues where *Embracing the Fear* leaves off. It delves deeper into the psychological factors that trigger anxiety and panic attacks. It stresses the importance of a healthy self-esteem, of setting boundaries, and feeling more in charge of our lives. Its content is more personal than the former book. It discusses approaches to journal writing and its value. It also answers readers' questions, such as *What about medication? Does acceptance mean that I can't do anything about my anxiety and I'll always have this problem? Isn't leaving a feared situation avoiding? Am I being negative by having low expectations?* It includes a chapter for support persons with suggestions on how they can help loved ones struggling with an anxiety disorder.

Written by a recovered agoraphobic, this book speaks from the heart. Those of us trying to cope with persistent and unexplainable anxiety or panic attacks need to be reminded that we are not alone, that someone else understands our plight. We need to know that there is hope for recovery. This book offers that hope. We discover, through coping strategies and gentle self-talk, that we no longer have to try so hard to fix or control our anxiety. That we no longer have to live in fear. A book reviewer once wrote about our program, "If you can imagine, there is no straining and striving to overcome your disorder, no 'hard work,' no guilt or shame, no pressure, no deadlines. The basic principle is a most permissive one, in a way that seems sensible, balanced and emotionally healthy."[2]

---

2 Encourage Newsletter, July/August 1994. Scottsdale, AZ. Written by Pat Merrill, Editor.

Organization

Chapter 1, *Origins*, recollects the early days of my agoraphobia, long before it was diagnosed. I share insights on the possible causes of my own disorder, as well as anxiety disorders in general. The emphasis is on change, separation and loss, repressed feelings, and low self-esteem. We learn how our emotions can play a significant role in anxiety. It helps if we can see the bigger picture, our common personality traits and the possible triggers for our anxiety and panic attacks.

Chapter 2, *The Power of Acceptance*, explores the various options we have for dealing with anxiety or panic by introducing helpful coping strategies, such as acceptance, permissive self-talk, allowing symptoms, slowing down, lowering expectations, and taking risks. We will learn the importance of keeping recovery open-ended and discuss the role of setbacks.

The exercises at the end of each strategy in chapter two are designed to help us become more aware of how we deal with our anxiety and how to deal with it more effectively. (However, it is not necessary to do the exercises to understand the concepts in this book.) The first exercise, *Taking a Look at Our Self-Talk*, helps us realize how we talk to ourselves when we are anxious. Then it introduces us to a more helpful inner dialogue. In the second exercise, *How Do We Cope?* we are asked to decide which strategies we would use in various situations. *More on Self-Talk* illustrates three different kinds of self-talk: one that is non-permissive and controlling, one that is rational but doesn't necessarily allow us to experience anxiety, and one that is gentle and permissive.

Chapter 3, *Acceptance in Everyday Life*, takes a look at different situations where we have difficulty, such as traveling, attending family gatherings, staying alone, or the workplace. Acceptance, the theme of this book, might seem too passive a strategy to have any effect on our anxiety, much less have the power to heal. It means *letting go* of control and that's the last thing we want to do. But *letting go and allowing* can make a significant difference in how we handle our anxiety and panic attacks. Acceptance is a concept that is often misunderstood. However, it will become more clear as we begin to see the bigger picture and work through each of the strategies. With repeated acceptance we will come to realize its power and its importance to our recovery. Exercises are included at the end of the chapter.

In Chapter 4, *Growing in Awareness*, we learn that recovery means more than being able to drive on the highway or shop at the mall without being anxious. Recovery means feeling more in charge of our lives by making decisions, being more assertive, and establishing boundaries. Recovery means having a healthier self-esteem. Becoming aware of what lies at the heart of our anxiety problem is invaluable because it helps us grow in self-confidence and regain independence.

Chapter 5, *Awareness through Journaling*, illustrates different ways we can journal. It explains how journal writing becomes an effective tool for expressing feelings and keeping track of helpful coping strategies. Over time, in spite of necessary setbacks, we see that we are still making progress in our recovery.

Chapter 6, *Beyond Acceptance*, focuses on self-care. It answers questions about exercise, relaxation and meditation, for example: Does exercise bring on physical symptoms? Why don't relaxation exercises always work for me? It discusses diaphragmatic breathing, bio-feedback and insomnia. It also answers questions that people with anxiety have about medication.

In *Parting Thoughts*, we look at the question, *What is recovery?* This same question was discussed in *Embracing the Fear*, but here, we view this subject from a personal perspective. I recount my final year in therapy and the insights I gained that eventually broke the anxiety–panic cycle. As my perception of the problem was changing, I no longer saw myself as a helpless victim. Pieces of the puzzle finally began to fall into place.

The final chapter, *Appendix*, is for the support person, whether family member or close friend. It answers many of their questions and suggests ways they can help the person with an anxiety or panic disorder. It also offers support and encouragement to the support person herself, who wants to be understanding but is often frustrated and discouraged.

Throughout the book you will read stories written by people like ourselves who are dealing with anxiety or panic attacks. These stories show that through the power of acceptance, they are willing to enter the places they fear. They have learned to have realistic expectations of themselves, use a kind of self-talk that is permissive of their anxiety and take their recovery out of a time frame. They go through setbacks that are such an important part of this process. Eventually, they come to understand the *meaning* of *acceptance* and are thereby able to move into a new comfort zone.

As a recovered agoraphobic, I know that we do not have to live with chronic anxiety or the constant fear of unpredictable panic attacks. I know that we can break through the fear, frustration, and isolation that we deal with on a daily basis. I know that we can move beyond the vulnerability and helplessness and take charge of our lives once again.

THE POWER OF ACCEPTANCE

CHAPTER ONE

ORIGINS

After having had so many panic attacks, why do I
still have to question what it is each time I have one?
Perhaps it's because they occur when I least expect them.
There doesn't seem to be any reason for them.

Journal entry
November, 1983

THE FIRST PANIC ATTACK

I remember myself as a young woman caught up in a whirlwind of activity, always on the go. In addition to a teaching career, I studied dance, sang in the community chorus and was active in community theater. Filled with a zest for life, I felt I had every reason to be happy.

I had just finished another year of teaching out of state and was getting ready to travel home for the summer. The upcoming months promised new beginnings. I would be taking graduate courses at the local university and living on campus. This meant being close to family and friends. Hopefully, I would find a teaching position closer to home and this would be my last trip between Michigan and Minnesota.

And then it happened. One day I was living life to its fullest and the next I was taking refuge in the safety of my apartment. Overwhelmed by sudden, unexplainable physical symptoms, I was convinced that I was dying. Afraid to walk outside my apartment door, I relied on my roommate to bring me meals from a nearby restaurant. This was the beginning of a long, perplexing nightmare. What was happening to me?

It was a Sunday morning in July that changed the course of my life. I was getting ready for church when I felt pressure in my chest. It wasn't severe, but uncomfortable enough to raise concern. As I left the house I tried to ignore it. But as I approached my destination, the symptoms multiplied. I began to feel light-headed, shaky. Breathing became uncomfortable. My hands perspired as I gripped the steering wheel. The thought suddenly occurred to me, *What if I'm having a heart attack?* I frantically tried to control the rising panic. I focused on my surroundings in an attempt to distract myself. I tried to be rational. But nothing worked.

I pulled into a service station and went to the phone booth, debating whether to dial 911. I felt completely cut off. I was consumed with a feeling of impending doom. *Am I going to die on this street corner?* Afraid to move from the phone booth in case I needed to call for help, I waited, desperately trying to control my erratic breathing. Time moved in slow motion, but my heart was racing. The panic reached its peak—and then subsided.

Feeling quite shaken, I gathered up every ounce of courage I had, got in my car and headed home. From there, I went to the emergency room where I spent the rest of the afternoon, only to be told that they couldn't find anything physically wrong with me. Rather than feeling relief, I became watchful over the next few days, anticipating another attack of the frightening symptoms.

The second episode came a week later.

My mother, sister and I had planned to visit relatives out of town. It was a two-hour drive. I was anxious about driving that far away from home. *What if I have that pressure in my chest again? What if I feel like I'm passing out somewhere on the highway where no one can help me?* And I certainly didn't want my mother to know that I was having a problem. It would only cause her worry.

As we started the trip, I tried to convince myself that I might not experience the frightening symptoms still hovering in the back of my mind. To make sure, I used every distraction. My mother and I talked as I drove. I concentrated hard on the conversation. I listened to the radio. I took in the scenery. But my thoughts raced frantically.

When we arrived at our destination, I breathed a sigh of relief. I had made the first part of the trip. But along with the sigh came the thought: *I still have to make it back home.* I was only at the halfway point. Going back would be worse because I had no choice. And having no choice, I would feel trapped.

We left the next day and headed north toward Minneapolis–St. Paul. I gripped the steering wheel hard and tried the same tactics I had used on the trip down. But to no avail. The continuous effort to distract myself—the sound of the radio and the desperate attempts to keep up a conversation—were no longer working. The panic escalated. The more I tried to control it the worse it got. I could no longer ignore the pressure in my chest. Hyperventilating and feeling as though I might pass out, I quickly pulled over to the side of the highway. My worst fear was coming true. I can still remember my mother waving down a passing car, waiting for the ambulance, the trip to the emergency room and the countless tests at the university hospital.

So began a pattern that would last for many years: constantly anticipating a panic attack, white-knuckling my way through a feared situation or avoiding it altogether, and carrying a shameful secret.

In the months that followed I became obsessed with my symptoms. I depended on friends and coworkers to drive me to and from work. My car sat in the driveway. This was all so new. Only twenty-four hours before my first episode I had felt fine. The symptoms came out of nowhere. Nothing unusual was happening. There were no outstanding stressors—certainly nothing that would cause feelings of such intensity.

Although the first attack took place in 1965, it wasn't until 1981 that I got a diagnosis: panic disorder with agoraphobia. Until that time I had been told repeatedly that it was "just nerves." During that sixteen-year period, I experienced many levels of anxiety. At times I didn't venture far from home; sometimes I didn't leave at all. There were times when I had two or three panic attacks a day, and then I would go for three or four months at a time when I was able to keep the panic attacks at bay. I would reach plateaus and then struggle through setbacks.

But in spite of the fear and intense discomfort, life went on and I wanted to be a part of it any way I could. I learned to endure the anxiety and panic symptoms and white-knuckle my way through life. I continued to teach, and eventually managed a social life of sorts. No one was aware of my inner struggle.

What went wrong? How did all this happen?

Through therapy, I learned that although stressful events can bring on panic, the attacks don't always happen immediately after an event. As time went on, I was able to trace the circumstances that led up to my first anxiety symptoms. I had broken an engagement two years before, had gone through surgery and was later hospitalized with a serious viral infection. During this time there was a death in the family. On top of this, I was still struggling with the idea of moving closer to home—a decision that involved not only a desire to be near family and friends, but also harbored feelings of guilt and emotional dependency. At the time of my first panic attack, I was enrolled in graduate courses at the university, which in itself was stressful. I felt overwhelmed.

Taking all of these factors into account, it's no wonder that the accumulating stress finally reached a point of overflowing. Author Robert Handly calls this the "rain barrel effect."[3] True, a broken relationship, medical issues, a death in the family, and making life changes were certainly a part of the problem. But it ran a lot deeper. Its roots had taken hold long before my first panic attack.

---

3 Handly, Robert. *Anxiety & Panic Attacks: Their Cause and Cure.* New York: Fawcett, 1987. page 37.

LOOKING AT THE PROBLEM

With our focus on genetic or biological causes, we might overlook
the psychological factors that underlie our anxiety or panic

During the years I struggled with panic disorder I was convinced that I was the only person on Earth with this problem. I felt totally alone. But once I started the Open Door support groups, I realized how far this was from the truth. I was amazed at the number of phone calls I received from people who had been diagnosed with an anxiety disorder. I began to think it was an epidemic.

Anxiety disorders are the most common psychiatric illnesses in the United States with 40 million adults (18.1%) affected. According to a study commissioned by the Anxiety Disorders Association of America and published in the *Journal of Clinical Psychiatry* (1999), anxiety disorders cost more than $42 billion a year, almost one-third of the $148 billion total mental health bill in the U.S.

People with an anxiety disorder are three to five times more likely to go to a doctor and six times more likely to be hospitalized for psychiatric disorders than non-sufferers. As with adults, anxiety disorders are the most common type of mental health disorder in children, affecting as many as ten percent of young people.[4]

In this chapter we look at the different anxiety disorders, explore possible causes, and discuss the personality traits common to people dealing with anxiety and panic attacks.

Anxiety Disorders

Most people who come to the Open Door support groups experience panic attacks (with or without agoraphobia), generalized anxiety, or social phobia. Others who benefit from this program have obsessive-compulsive disorder (OCD) and post-traumatic stress disorder (PTSD), both of which involve significant anxiety. Six anxiety disorders are briefly described below.[5]

Panic Disorder With Agoraphobia is the most common and most debilitating of the anxiety disorders. Those with PDA experience recurring panic attacks that seem to come from out of the blue. A fear of being trapped and unable to get help results in the tendency to avoid places where panic might occur.

Panic Disorder Without Agoraphobia is similar to PDA except for the extensive avoidance. Recurrent and unexpected panic attacks cause constant concern.

Social Phobia involves intense anxiety brought on by certain social or performance situations. There is a fear of humiliating or embarrassing oneself.

---

4 Source: Anxiety Disorders Association of America web site. www.adaa.org.
5 Bemis, Judith and Amr Barrada. *Embracing the Fear: Learning to Manage Anxiety and Panic Attacks.* Center City: Hazelden Publications, 1994. pages 4-5.

Obsessive-Compulsive Disorder is characterized by intrusive thoughts that cause marked anxiety and/or repetitive behaviors that appear to be done to relieve the anxiety.

Posttraumatic Stress Disorder is characterized by the reexperiencing of a traumatic event. The person with PTSD experiences increased anxiety and depression, and attempts to avoid activities or situations associated with the trauma.

Generalized Anxiety Disorder is characterized by persistent anxiety over a long period of time. The person with GAD feels that their problems are difficult to manage and that they have little control over them.

Defining a Panic Attack

I nearly panicked! People who use this expression may have no idea what they are saying.

Generally speaking, a real panic attack comes on suddenly and without warning. It can happen anywhere and any time. Since the symptoms often bear no resemblance to anxiety, panic sufferers might think they are passing out or that they are having a heart attack or stroke. Others are afraid they are going crazy. Many think they are going to make a fool of themselves. There is an overwhelming sense of danger and thus an urgent need to escape from the situation.

In physiological terms, what is happening? When faced with danger, nature has a way of protecting us. It is called the fight-or-flight response. The brain releases hormones that constrict the blood vessels in the arms, legs, and hands. This drives the blood into the brain as well as into the large muscles to increase strength. The heart pounds, the breathing rate increases, and the muscles tighten.[6] What makes it so frightening for us is that we experience the fight-or-flight response when there is no *immediate* danger. With panic, we are caught off guard, suddenly and unexpectedly.

People experience a variety of symptoms during a panic attack. If you have four or more of the following symptoms (see below) at one time, you are probably experiencing panic. In any case, it is always best to consult a professional for an accurate diagnosis. Common symptoms of a panic attack include:[7]

- increased heart rate
- dizziness or light-headedness, faintness
- increased respiration
- trembling hands or legs, weak knees
- shortness of breath, a feeling of suffocation
- difficulty swallowing
- confusion, inability to concentrate
- a feeling of unreality (depersonalization)
- blurred vision
- chest pain or discomfort
- nausea or abdominal distress

---

6 Handly, *Anxiety & Panic Attacks,* page 22.
7 Bemis, Judith and Amr Barrada, *Embracing the Fear,* page 4.

- fear of dying
- fear of going crazy
- a sense of impending doom

No matter what the particular symptoms, a panic attack can leave us feeling terrified, isolated and desperately in need of help.

Why Am I Panicking?

One of the first questions we ask ourselves is, why do I have this problem? We can spend a lot of time trying to find the answer, but there isn't one simple answer, nor are the answers the same for everyone. According to Edmund J. Bourne, author of *The Anxiety & Phobia Workbook*, "there is no single cause, and such a theory tends to oversimplify anxiety disorders." He goes on to say that "anxiety problems are brought about by a variety of causes operating on numerous different levels. These levels include heredity, biology, family background and upbringing, conditioning, recent stressors, your self-talk and personal belief system, your ability to express feelings, and so on."[8]

When I first started facilitating anxiety support groups, I often asked myself, what do these people have in common other than their anxiety or panic attacks? The groups are made up of both men and women from all walks of life: students, educators, housewives, and businessmen and women. They have many fine qualities. They

---

8 Bourne, Edmund J. *The Anxiety & Phobia Workbook*. Oakland: New Harbinger Publications, 1990. page 21.

are often high achievers, conscientious, caring and sensitive. In searching for a common thread I also discovered that many have certain personality traits in common. They often lack assertiveness. They have low self-esteem and a high need for approval. They are perfectionists. They tend to be chronic worriers, and although sensitive to criticism, they are very critical of themselves.

Panic Attacks and Heredity

Another question that comes up for us is whether anxiety disorders are inherited.

It is not unusual for several members of one family to experience panic attacks. Studies of families with panic disorder and studies of identical twins suggest, in fact, that our vulnerability to anxiety disorders is most likely inherited. For example, an early study found that identical twins who share 100 percent of their genes are more likely to share panic disorder than nonidentical twins who share only 50 percent of their genes.[9]

I hadn't thought about a genetic link in my own family until one day when my sister and I started talking about our trip to southern Minnesota in the summer of 1965 when I had one of my first panic attacks. She remembered how frightened our mother was—waving down passing cars, waiting for the ambulance. My sister asked her what was wrong. The answer, simple and direct, came as a total shock: "It's hereditary." No further explanation was

---

9 Beckfield, Denise. *Master Your Panic & Take Back Your Life!* Atascadero, Calif.: Impact Publishers, 1994. page 21.

ever given. Thirty-one years after the event I heard something that I had never heard before. Why wasn't I told? And who in my family had this problem?

With a family history of panic disorder, the chances of inheriting it are between ten and fifteen percent. With no family history, the chances are between two and five percent.[10] According to Edmund Bourne, "Based on what is known at this time, it seems that you don't inherit agoraphobia, social phobia or even panic attacks specifically from your parents. What is inherited seems to be a general personality type that predisposes you to be overly anxious." He goes on to say, "Once you are born with this highly reactive personality, you might develop one or another anxiety disorder depending on your particular environment and upbringing."[11]

With this in mind, we might wonder, did our parents or guardians have unrealistic expectations of us? Were they highly critical, not allowing for any mistakes? Were they over-protective, continually expressing worry and concern? Was there any neglect or abuse? How did they, themselves, deal with stress? These questions are well worth considering because the answers can be directly related to an anxiety problem.

However, it does not matter whether an anxiety disorder is genetic, environmental, or a combination of both. The good news is that anxiety is *treatable* and that *recovery is possible*. Unfortunately, those who believe that our anxiety is strictly biological or genetic

---

10 Beckfield, *Master Your Panic*, page 22.
11 Bourne, *Anxiety & Phobia Workbook*, page 24.

tend to think that nothing can be done about it. This belief leaves us open to feeling helpless. However, we are not victims. We can do something to help ourselves.

Other Factors to Consider

Along with genetic causes, other factors may underlie our anxiety or panic attacks as well. As mentioned earlier, those of us dealing with an anxiety or panic disorder have certain personality traits in common. We might want to consider the following: Instead of always seeing things in black or white, perhaps we need to see more gray. Perhaps we need to recognize our need for perfection. Maybe it would help to become more aware of how we tend to magnify problems or events. Or maybe it's a matter of putting balance into our lives by slowing down and taking better care of ourselves both physically and emotionally. There are so many contributing factors to consider that it seems unlikely that anxiety and panic attacks could appear out of the blue or that they are strictly hereditary. If we think carefully and honestly about the following questions, we can gain important insights into what lies beneath our anxiety and panic attacks. Professional therapy can deepen this awareness.

Do I tend to see things in black or white?

Many of us need to see more gray areas in our lives. Chances are, we didn't learn about gray areas when we were growing up. We learned that something was either right or wrong, good or bad. In elementary and middle school, we either made the grade or we didn't, and there were plenty of opportunities to compare our academic (or athletic) skills with those of our classmates. If *we* didn't make the comparisons, they did. And it didn't stop there. When we went on to high school and college, the competition increased. This either–or thinking continues to create a lot of anxiety for us since it leaves us with no options. In the following story Kent writes about his fast-paced world of black-or-white thinking.

Kent's Story

I recently ran across a paper I wrote for a college psychology class entitled, "Self-Concept." I wrote about my high school and college days and how I struggled with self-confidence. I see now that I failed to appreciate my own accomplishments. After graduation, new challenges awaited me. A successful career boosted my self-confidence, but I set my expectations unreasonably high. I worked long hours and my performance standards were often unrealistic. Living in my own fast-paced world, I allowed little time for myself. Life was a pattern of set rules with no exceptions. There was no room for mistakes, no matter how small: making a mistake was a direct attack on my self-worth. Anxious to please, I hadn't learned about boundaries and how important they were in maintaining a healthy self-esteem. A year after this paper was written, I started having panic attacks. As I look back at this assignment, I can see how my lack of self-confidence, my fast-paced lifestyle and black-or-white thinking were a major part of my anxiety problem.

Do I have unrealistic expectations of myself?

Our perfectionism and all-or-nothing thinking can distort the way we see ourselves and our accomplishments. Words like "always" and "never" are common in our vocabulary. No matter what we do, it is never good enough. We exhaust ourselves trying to live up to our unrealistic standards. We don't give ourselves a break, recognizing that sometimes we make mistakes. We overlook the fact that mistakes are part of being human. A supportive, nurturing self-talk can help to reassure us that we do not have to be perfect: *It's okay for me to make mistakes.* We need to let go of our perfectionism, as difficult as that may be. Otherwise nothing we do will ever meet our standards.

Do I have a tendency to magnify problems or mistakes?

Some people can make a mistake, learn from it, and then go on with their lives. For many of us that is often not the case. We can go for days berating ourselves over some seemingly unforgivable error. Rather than seeing the larger picture, we can take even the smallest mistake and blow it out of proportion. This is illustrated in the following account of a choral program I once presented.

Judy's Story

My elementary school chorus gave a concert for the staff

and student body. Halfway through one of the songs the children suddenly rushed ahead of the accompaniment tape. I felt out of control of the situation, but kept on directing. After the performance, I had a difficult time working through my disappointment. They had sung ten songs and yet I obsessed over this one piece as though the success of the whole concert depended on it. It made no difference how well the rest of the program went: I felt that the concert was a failure. It was days before I could finally stop obsessing over a mistake that simply shouldn't have happened.

Later that week I ran into a colleague at a local store. "I have to tell you," she said. "The concert was absolutely marvelous. The tone was beautiful. And the diction? I could understand every word. It was wonderful!" I was really taken by surprise. Was it possible that she hadn't noticed the blunder, the unforgivable error that I was sure had ruined the whole concert? I was tempted to point out her oversight, but decided to let it go. I was simply amazed at how hard I am on myself, how I can obsess over my every mistake.

Seeing the whole program as a failure because of one error is a prime example of magnifying or "catastrophizing" an event. There was no way I could enjoy feeling good about the concert's overall success. No wonder my anticipatory anxiety was always so high before performances: I knew the price I would have to pay for a less than perfect outcome.

What can Trigger Anxiety or Panic?

In *The First Panic Attack* I wrote about the events that led up to my first encounter with panic: a broken engagement, surgery, illness, a death in the family, a decision to move closer to home, and plans to attend graduate school, all of which caused me a great deal of stress. By answering the following questions you might gain a better understanding of what triggered, or continues to trigger, your anxiety or panic attacks.

How do I deal with change?

Change in any form can trigger anxiety in our lives, whether it's a new job, moving to a new home, a new relationship, or a change in our health. Even a variation in our daily routine can affect our sense of well-being. Afraid of change, we strive to maintain the status quo. We find security in the familiar.

In the wake of change, we can sometimes lose our sense of purpose. The empty nester, the widow or widower, the retiree, the person laid off and between jobs—all can feel as though they are drifting. Having purpose gives life meaning. We need something to look forward to and get excited about. Even feel passionate about. Without purpose, we can experience an increased level of anxiety.

As a teacher, I had a difficult time adjusting to summer vacations. It meant getting off my treadmill, changing my routine, and having more unstructured time on my hands. It was as though my desk at school was my life raft and I had to return to it on a regular basis to maintain my identity. During June I had little or no problem.

In July I started to notice some anxiety. With the heat of August, my panic attacks would resurface and I longed for the structure of the coming school year. I knew that I would once again thrive on the flurry of activity that the end of the long summer months would bring, and find purpose in the familiar routines of lesson planning, committee responsibilities, and meaningful interaction with my students.

As we grow older, change can take on new dimensions. Our family structure changes when parents or spouse die, children grow up and move away, and grandchildren are born. When colleagues retire, we may feel we are losing our past. Our need for the familiar makes change difficult for us. In fact, it can hold us back from making changes that could improve our lives or add joy to everyday living.

Do I have a history of loss?

Separation and loss can bring dramatic change. One study shows that many adults suffering from agoraphobia experienced separation anxiety as children, usually from the mother or both parents.[12] Looking back, I can trace a history of separation anxiety in my own life.

Judy's Story

My father died when I was very young. My widowed mother, brother and I, lived with our grandparents. I never quite

---

12 Beckfield, *Master Your Panic*, pages 23-24.

understood why other kids had a dad and I didn't. Although I never talked about my feelings I was painfully aware that he was not a part of my life. My mother worked—at a time when most mothers didn't—and I was aware of her absence as well. Looking back, I am struck by the fact that we rarely talked about my father. This only added to the void that I was feeling. A small wooden chest that he had made would surface from time to time. It contained a few precious keepsakes that gave me a sense of connection with an unknown past. Although little was said, I did think about him. I felt cheated that I never really knew the sound of his voice, had no memory of his smile, nor had I even a gesture by which to remember him. My mother remarried and moved away when I was ten. I continued to stay with my grandmother. When she died I lived in fear of losing my mother as well.

Emotional dependency grows from such experiences, as well as vulnerability to future loss. However, according to Beckfield, "Loss or separation needn't actually occur for people to develop fears about loss, fears that underlie panic."[13]

Losing someone special in our lives is one kind of loss. There is also lost youth that must be dealt with or letting go of unfulfilled dreams. Perhaps in our disillusionment, our disappointment

---

13 Beckfield, *Master Your Panic,* page 24.

of dreams never realized, we've stopped dreaming altogether. This, in itself, is a substantial loss, since when we no longer have dreams, we tend to give up.

No one is free from the pain of separation or loss. Sooner or later, we all experience feelings of emptiness. What is important is how we deal with our feelings. Do we work through them over time or do we quietly move into denial because they're just too painful to deal with? Unfortunately, many of us choose the latter as a way of coping. And therein lies one of our problems: repressing feelings causes more stress and anxiety.

Do I have a history of abuse?
Coming from an abusive or dysfunctional background does not necessarily result in an anxiety disorder. However, it is not uncommon to hear anxiety sufferers refer to a history of abuse. Many of us were victims of alcoholism. We grew up in an environment where we had little control of our circumstances, where we learned to walk on pins and needles, not knowing what to expect next. We learned to live in fear. Denial and avoidance became ways of coping with situations we felt were out of our control. Such coping strategies became a way of survival.

Because of this dysfunctional environment of alcoholism and abuse, we learned to avoid conflict at all costs. Feeling powerless because we couldn't change our circumstances, we convinced ourselves that our problems were not that important and it was better to just ignore them. That way, we didn't have to deal with them.

We were told to be strong and tough it out. Self-pity simply was not acceptable.

Putting up a brave front, we overlooked some of our basic rights, for example, the right to feel loved, to be accepted or appreciated, to feel good about ourselves, to be respected, and to have a sense of belonging. We overlooked the fact that *we have the right to feel safe.* It is easy for life to get out of balance when we are constantly struggling against circumstances we cannot control, when our focus is on emotional survival.

In the following story, we see how Jenna learned to live in fear in a dysfunctional family environment.

Jenna's Story

I dreaded weekends when I was a teenager. My parents went out Saturday nights and I would babysit my younger brother. After going to bed I would lie awake in the darkness of my room, waiting. Well past midnight, I would hear the car pull into the driveway. Just hearing the back screen door open made my muscles tighten and then start to convulse. The anxiety was that intense. I knew my parents had been drinking and the best I could hope for was no violent arguments. I made sure I stayed awake until they both were asleep.

I first noticed some light-headedness and a sense of foreboding during these years. I carried smelling salts to school every day, afraid I would pass out in class and embarrass myself in front of the other kids. I felt trapped in a home situation I couldn't escape. I was miserable, but at the same time I didn't feel I had the right to complain. No one, not even my close friends, knew how unhappy I was, or what went on in that house.

Do I have low self-esteem?

Self-esteem is the image we have of ourselves, and how we feel about that image. It is a deep sense of self-worth and well-being that is essential to our happiness. According to Edmund Bourne, low self-esteem is among the deepest of all the contributing causes of anxiety disorders.[14] Many people suffer from low self-esteem, even those who are successful. That is because reality isn't necessarily what determines how we feel, but our *perception* of reality. For example, no matter how successful we are, we must *believe* we are successful.

What causes low self-esteem? Earlier, we cited the critical parent or caregiver who didn't allow us to make mistakes or was overprotective. We also discussed the dysfunctional family environment, in which there was abuse or neglect. Living with alcoholism, for example, is a prime setting for emotional abuse. Subject to repeated episodes of bizarre and often cruel behavior, we lose sight of what is normal. We try to cover up the dysfunction and the shame it brings on, yet our emotional well-being is damaged. The following story illustrates how emotional abuse can affect self-esteem.

---

14 Bourne, *Anxiety & Phobia Workbook,* page 48.

Jenna's Story

In high school I was quiet and withdrawn. Working at a part-time job, I never engaged in after-school activities. At home, my alcoholic father ignored me. Days would go by and he wouldn't look at me or speak to me. I remember feeling invisible. I wasn't sure what was worse—the silence when he was sober or the verbal abuse when he was drinking. Either way, it was cruel and demeaning. I tried to ignore his humiliating remarks and learned to avoid him whenever possible.

Because of his violent behavior when drinking, I feared for my mother's safety and focused on protecting her. Perhaps this was a way of minimizing my own emotional pain. The panic attacks started during my sophomore year. They let up before the end of the school year, but returned in my mid-twenties.

But even if we come from a background that was detrimental to our self-worth and well-being, all is not lost. We can still take steps to regain or improve our self-esteem; we can still move ahead with our lives. Realizing what we've had to deal with, we can embrace ourselves with compassion and begin using a nurturing self-talk based on acceptance. This will not be an easy task. Our harsh, critical self-talk has been a part of us for a long time. But if we accept ourselves, we can allow mistakes and start to focus on our positive attributes.

Taking risks is another way of improving our self-esteem. However, because our self-esteem is so fragile, we will go to great lengths to protect it. Rather than add to our list of failures, we avoid taking risks altogether. But risk-taking is important: it helps to build self-confidence. Self-confidence leads to taking more risks and to the successes that are so valuable to our self-esteem. I found this to be true when I applied for graduate school.

Judy's Story

I was in a Transactional Analysis support group at the time. At one of our meetings, I voiced my desire to continue my education, but said I was afraid of being turned down. Applying for graduate school meant taking a huge risk. Our group leader responded, "I want you to mail in your application before our next meeting."

Seeing this as a challenge, I took him up on it—and got accepted. Yet this risk was just the first of many that I would take over the next two years. Unlike my undergraduate education, I made a point of knowing my instructors, got involved in class discussions, and took leadership roles. I felt a renewed sense of accomplishment and a new self-confidence. In spite of the stresses—long hours of study, written exams and reports—I was free of panic attacks. But only in retrospect could I understand the connection. Applying for graduate school was one of the best things I ever did for my self-esteem.

But I'm not under any stress right now

Anxiety and panic attacks can occur even when everything in our life seems to be going well. That's because there can be a delayed reaction to stressful events. It was six months to a year after going through a stressful period in my life before I had my first panic attack. Considering this potential time lapse, it is no wonder we are bewildered by our symptoms and think they are coming out of the blue.

With the help of a professional therapist we can discover what triggers our anxiety and panic attacks and better understand what lies at the heart of the problem. This awareness can make it easier to be more accepting of our situation; it will keep us from feeling overwhelmed. Although it seems mysterious, the anxiety is there for a reason. It is trying to tell us something. An anxiety disorder has a way of stopping us in our tracks, of getting us to sit up and take notice. Once in its grasp we can no longer rely on minimization, avoidance and denial—our old coping strategies. At this point, it might help to evaluate how well we're dealing with the problem areas in our lives and, if necessary, find ways to deal with them more effectively.

If I find out what is causing my anxiety, will it go away?

We sometimes think that if we could just resolve a particular conflict or make an important decision, such as changing jobs or ending a relationship, we would no longer have an anxiety problem. Although such resolution is important and can make a significant difference in our anxiety level, it usually isn't that simple. In my case, it wasn't any particular problem that triggered my anxiety, but how I dealt with problems in general. I thought that moving to a new location would put an end to my anxiety symptoms, but I ended up taking my anxiety and panic attacks with me. As new problems surfaced, I continued to deal with them in my usual way—minimization, avoidance, and denial.

If we didn't look at the emotional or psychological side of our anxiety problem we would miss the opportunity to grow in self-awareness. We would pass up the chance to gain a better understanding of ourselves and how we deal (or don't deal) with problems in our lives. Our anxiety can take on a whole new light when we see it has changed our lives for the better. Robert Handly writes, "Now I can say that the day I had my first panic attack was the best day of my life."[15] Because of his panic attacks, he had to look at his lifestyle and see what needed to change. His panic disorder forced him to find a way to deal with his anxiety and panic.

Points to Remember: *Looking at the Problem*

1. Anxiety disorders are caused by a variety of factors operating on different levels. These factors include heredity, biology, family background and upbringing, conditioning, recent stressors, self-talk, our personal belief system, and our ability to express feelings.[16]

---

15 Handly, *Anxiety & Panic Attacks,* page 35.
16 Bourne, *Anxiety & Phobia Workbook,* page 21.

2. People with anxiety disorders have certain personality traits in common: We tend to be perfectionists. We are often passive and have a high need for approval. We tend to be chronic worriers, and although sensitive to criticism, we can be very critical of ourselves.

3. Low self-esteem is among the fundamental causes of anxiety disorders.[17]

4. Many anxiety sufferers have a history of abuse. Denial and avoidance became ways of coping with situations we felt were out of our control.

5. Change in any form—job, home, relationships, health and others—can trigger anxiety. Even a change in daily routine can affect our sense of well-being.

6. Our perfectionism and all-or-nothing thinking can distort how we see ourselves and our accomplishments.

7. We tend to magnify our mistakes. We can take the smallest error and turn it into a catastrophe.

8. Anxiety and panic attacks can occur even when everything in our life seems to be going well, since there can be a delayed reaction to stressful events.

9. Even if we come from a background that was detrimental to our self-worth and well-being, all is not lost. We can still take steps to improve our self-esteem and move forward with our lives.

---

17 Bourne, *Anxiety & Phobia Workbook,* page 48.

CHAPTER TWO

THE POWER OF ACCEPTANCE

I just don't understand why I'm feeling this way.
I'm at a point where I'm taking one day at a time.
There has to be a way out. I seem to go from acceptance
to despair. What is this freedom I long for?
What are these prison walls protecting me from?

Journal entry
June, 1984

THE MEANING OF ACCEPTANCE

It's the accepting, the surrendering to our anxiety
that can break the anxiety–panic cycle

T he power of acceptance is a challenging concept for those of us who feel trapped in a cycle of fear. Perhaps the notion of *accepting* or *allowing* seems too simple a strategy for dealing with anxiety or panic attacks. Seeing the problem as complex, we look for complex answers. However, I repeatedly hear people say, "The thing that helped me the most in my recovery was acceptance." Despite its effectiveness in breaking the anxiety–panic cycle, accepting seems contrary to what we think we *should* be doing, that is, trying hard to control our anxiety symptoms. However, this need to control only builds up a resistance, which, in itself, creates a problem.

According to Reid Wilson,[18] a psychologist who specializes in the treatment of anxiety disorders, whenever we resist something it will persist because we have created a polarity (opposing forces). He gives the following example: Two hundred warriors are marching toward us. What do we do? Attack or retreat? We are told that either

---

18 Wilson, Reid. *Don't Panic: Taking Control of Anxiety Attacks.* New York: Harper & Row, 1996. page 244.

will provoke an aggressive response. On the other hand, if we do nothing but sit and observe, we will not attract their attention.

The same holds true for the onset of panic. The greater the resistance, the greater the chance of a full-blown attack. And by becoming a passive observer—that is, allowing the symptoms without fighting them—we lessen the chance of panic occurring. However, acceptance does not mean just *putting up with* or *tolerating* the anxiety symptoms, thinking there is nothing we can do about them anyway.

Acceptance means giving ourselves permission to be anxious or to experience panic attacks rather than resist them. Acceptance means allowing ourselves to have an anxiety problem

How do I know when I'm accepting my anxiety?
Tuning in to our self-talk is one way of knowing whether we are accepting our anxiety. What are we saying about it? If we are telling ourselves that we shouldn't have this problem or that we have to get rid of the anxiety we are not accepting. Instead, we are trying hard to control our symptoms. However, we need to allow them to run their course.

At a support group meeting, someone once commented, "I understand the concepts we're discussing—acceptance and allowing the sensations of panic. I really think I'm doing that. So, why am I still panicking?" She then went on to say, "Each time I feel the anxiety building I say to myself, *Oh, dear! Here it is again. How long is this going to go on?"* This inner dialogue tells us why her panic attacks are continuing. Still feeling overwhelmed, she is merely putting up with her symptoms while desperately hoping to get rid of them as soon as possible. Even when some of us think we are accepting our anxiety, we don't always realize what we are saying to ourselves and the difference our self-talk can make.

Does acceptance mean I'm always going to have this problem?
"I'm having a difficult time with the idea of acceptance," said another support group member. "I feel that if I give in to my anxiety or accept it, it will continue to get worse and I'll always have it. Many of us think that if we don't put a stop to the anxiety or panic it will get worse. However, fear of being unable to control the anxiety and the anticipation of it getting worse play a big part in perpetuating the problem. It's the accepting, the surrendering to our anxiety and panic symptoms—*not* fighting them—that can help break the anxiety–panic cycle. While acceptance on a long-term basis may seem overwhelming, if not impossible, trying to accept our anxiety one day at a time is more realistic and achievable.

What does it mean to say that I don't have to do anything
about my anxiety?
In *Embracing the Fear* we read that "Nowhere in the program are we told that we must do something about our anxiety, such as getting rid of it or controlling it."[19] Does this mean we sit back and pretend

---

19 Bemis, Judith and Amr Barrada, *Embracing the Fear,* page 17.

we don't have a problem? No. By *accepting, allowing, and letting go* we *are* doing something about our problem. It is the *controlling* and *trying hard to fix* our anxiety that is problematic because it can be self-defeating. For example, we continually tell ourselves that we have to be in control. Or we force ourselves into difficult situations where we feel anxious—*I have to stop being so anxious. What's wrong with me? This isn't normal*—and thus reinforce the anxiety with nonpermissive self-talk. Or we avoid those same situations and then feel shame for doing so. We are frustrated in our attempts, but determined to rid ourselves of our problem. Yet we don't consider *acceptance* an option. After all, it seems only logical that we should try to stop such unacceptable feelings. But trying so hard to get rid of our anxiety, or feeling that we have to control it, work against us: a resistance builds up.

I've tried everything, but nothing seems to work
We may find ourselves looking for answers in every direction and feeling as though we're getting nowhere. Frustrated and discouraged, we try even harder to find relief from our anxiety or panic attacks. We go from one doctor or therapist to another, looking for the right treatment or medication. We read every book on the subject we can get hold of, hoping to find that one sentence—or that one word—that will make the difference. We try relaxation and breathing exercises, recite positive affirmations—and give up when we don't get immediate results. We constantly search for the magic cure.

The issue is not that we try any of these approaches. All can be useful. The issue is that we are approaching our recovery with the same perfectionism that was part of the problem in the first place: high expectations and a self-talk that does not allow failure.

A visiting therapist once began a support group meeting by announcing to the group, "You are okay just the way you are. You don't have to change anything." I sensed a feeling of relief throughout the room. "It was wonderful!" exclaimed a group member after the meeting. "It was the first time anyone ever made me feel okay about my anxiety. It was like having a weight taken off my shoulders."

The speaker's message was that we need to give ourselves permission to be anxious. *Acceptance* is the key word. By taking off the internal pressure—*I have to do something to get rid of this anxiety!*—we can go about our recovery at our own pace and on our own terms, in a way that is gentle and less demanding.

We might want to remind ourselves that on some days acceptance will be easier than on others. And it will help to be accepting of *that* too. But with time, knowing that we no longer have to fight our anxiety or panic attacks, we can say to ourselves: *This is how it is for now. So be it!* According to Claire Weekes, "You repeat acceptance and see its effect on your symptoms so often, you finally lose your fear of them; you see acceptance work so often you come to understand and believe in it.[20]

---

20 Weekes, *Simple, Effective Treatment of Agoraphobia*, page 113.

In the following story we see how Debby fought her anxiety problem by trying to wish it away. Over time she comes to accept her agoraphobia and sees it as a positive experience.

Debby's Story

During the darkest days of my agoraphobia, I often wished that I had some physical illness. Anything would have been better than to be so afraid of living day by day in a constant state of panic. I would rationalize that at least people with physical illnesses could go places where I couldn't. I was sure that they were not afraid to stand alone in grocery store lines or walk around the block without having a panic attack or needing that "safe person" with them. Many times I found myself praying for something other than this terrible panic that made me feel so dependent and alone.

Now that I am in recovery I feel very fortunate that I have only agoraphobia. "Only" is not a word I use lightly nor take for granted. I say "only" because there is a way out of agoraphobia and I am on the road of recovery. I have spent many hours in fear and in tears wondering if I would ever be "normal" again. Twenty years ago, by the grace of God, I came from New York to live in Minnesota. I will soon return to New York as a different person. I will be returning with all the knowledge I have gained through my support groups, newsletters, therapists and all my friends. I have learned that my safe person resides within me. I have developed an inner strength that was always there (but had somehow lost the way to find it). I've learned to nurture the scared little girl inside of me instead of wishing she would disappear. Through this agoraphobia, I have found a woman who has become my best friend. This woman is myself and I like her. I have allowed my feelings to be a part of who I am instead of denying their existence. I have learned through cognitive therapy to connect these feelings with thoughts, making them less frightening. By giving myself permission to have my fears, I have set them free.

Since this was written, Debby earned her degree in social work with a minor in psychology.

Points to Remember: *Acceptance*

1. *Acceptance* is a key word in our recovery. It means giving ourselves permission to be anxious or to experience panic attacks rather than resisting them.

2. There's a difference between accepting and tolerating our anxiety and panic attacks. Tolerating means merely putting up with our symptoms, hoping they will go away. Acceptance means allowing ourselves to have an anxiety problem and feeling okay about ourselves in spite of it.

3. Rather than trying so hard to fix our anxiety or change how we feel, it is more helpful to change our perception of what is happening to us.

4. The fear of not being able to control our anxiety and the anticipation of it getting worse play a big part in perpetuating the problem.

5. We know we are trying too hard when we find ourselves looking for answers in every which direction and end up feeling like we're getting nowhere.

6. We approach recovery with the same perfectionism that was part of the problem in the first place: with high expectations and a nonpermissive self-talk.

7. It will help if we can go about our recovery at our own pace and on our own terms in a way that is gentle and more permissive.

Taking a Closer Look at Our Self-Talk
When I first notice the sensation of anxiety or panic starting to build up, what messages do I give myself?

1. Do I try to control the anxiety or panic in ways other than my self-talk? If so, how?

2. What might I say to myself to help deal with my anxiety and panic attacks more effectively and to be more accepting of them?
(See suggested answers on page 42.)

How Do We Cope? *At the Coffee Shop*
What strategies would you use in the following situation?
You are having coffee with a friend. You suddenly feel very anxious and anticipate a panic attack. You want to leave, but you're afraid to tell your friend how you are feeling for fear of alarming her or embarrassing yourself. *(See suggested answers on page 42.)*

More on Self-Talk: *Acceptance*

What Am I Really Saying to Myself?

Here are three examples of how we might talk to ourselves at the onset of a panic attack. Example 1 shows how we typically respond when we feel anxious. Example 2 is a rational, logical response—attempting to fix or change how we are feeling. But with example 3 we are accepting the anxiety or panic by allowing it to happen.

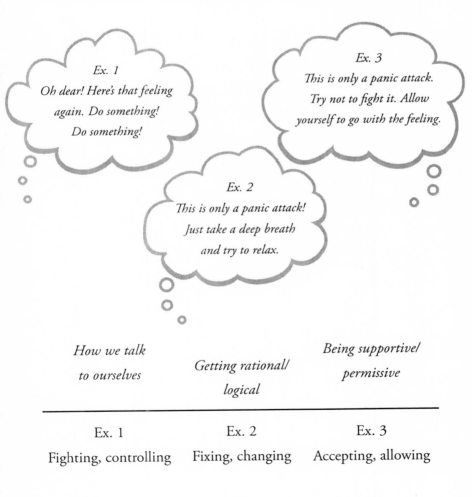

Ex. 1
Oh dear! Here's that feeling again. Do something! Do something!

Ex. 3
This is only a panic attack. Try not to fight it. Allow yourself to go with the feeling.

Ex. 2
This is only a panic attack! Just take a deep breath and try to relax.

How we talk to ourselves	*Getting rational/ logical*	*Being supportive/ permissive*
Ex. 1	Ex. 2	Ex. 3
Fighting, controlling	Fixing, changing	Accepting, allowing

(Suggested answers from page 40.)

Taking a Closer Look at Our Self-Talk (question #2)

1. It will help if I give myself permission to be anxious.

2. It's only a panic attack. If it happens, it happens.

3. This is how I am feeling today. So be it.

4. This is how I react to this kind of situation. It's okay to have these feelings. I do not have to feel embarrassed or ashamed.

How Do We Cope? At the Coffee Shop

Strategy A: I can float through the anxiety, letting it run its course. I know that I have the option to leave, but I choose to stay and say nothing to my friend about how I'm feeling.

Strategy B: I can tell my friend that I sometimes feel anxious in public places, and tell her not to be concerned if I should get up to leave for a little while.

THE GENTLE VOICE WITHIN: SELF-TALK

As I learn an inner dialogue that allows me to experience my
anxiety or panic attacks, they tend to lose their power

I t was a harsh, critical, and nonpermissive self-talk that continually undermined my self-esteem and imposed unrealistic
expectations; it was a self-talk that lay at the heart of my anxiety
problem. In time, I would learn an inner dialogue that challenged
my former beliefs, a self-talk that would nourish and sustain me,
and play a dominant role in my recovery.

To manage our anxiety, we need to better recognize how we
talk to ourselves and how that "self-talk" affects our anxiety. In this
section, we will read about three different types of inner dialogue:
one that is harsh, critical and nonpermissive (it doesn't allow us to
be anxious); one that is logical or rational; and one that is permissive, gentle and nurturing.

What is a nurturing and supportive self-talk?
Let us try to imagine an inner voice that allows all the fear and anxiety that we are now struggling with; a voice that takes us to a place
of total acceptance. Of all the strategies we use in dealing with our

anxiety or panic attacks, a supportive and nurturing self-talk is at the top of the list. Our inner dialogue constantly gives us messages about how we feel about our anxiety and panic attacks. Those messages play a significant part in how we react in feared situations and how we feel about ourselves as anxiety and panic sufferers.

Nurturing and supportive self-talk is gentle and permissive of our thoughts, actions and feelings. It is not harsh, demeaning, or critical

If we were to say to ourselves, *I hate this anxiety! I wish it would just go away*, a supportive counterstatement would be, *Of course I don't like how I'm feeling. But it will help if I can allow myself to be anxious.* In this way, we acknowledge our true feelings about our anxiety, and at the same time remind ourselves that allowing our symptoms is a more helpful way of dealing with them.

Learning a compassionate self-talk, based on acceptance, was vital to my own recovery. It didn't happen right away. It took time, patience, and practice. Through cognitive therapy, I learned to listen to the way I was talking to myself. I kept hearing a voice that was harsh and unforgiving, a voice that demanded perfection and recorded every failure. My therapist called this "A-talk."[21]

Judy's Story

As far back as I can remember I was an "A-talker." I just

---

21 Bemis and Barrada, *Embracing the Fear*, page 31.

never realized how it affected my life. It was a self-talk that contributed to my anxiety disorder, and continued to sustain it. Trying to control my symptoms, my self-talk was telling me to pull myself together and do something about my problem. Over time I learned a new way of talking to myself, one that was more permissive of my anxiety and panic. It was called B-talk. During my recovery, I continued to use A-talk, but to a lesser degree. My B-talk was talking back. I actually had a dialogue going between them. I was giving myself permission to be anxious, to leave uncomfortable situations when necessary, and even allow the terrifying symptoms of a panic attack. After a while, I was talking to my panic as though it were an old friend. *You're back! Here you are again! So what else is new?*

I began using a nurturing self-talk in other areas of my life, too, which furthered my recovery. My inner voice was becoming less self-critical. In other words, it was giving me permission to be myself.

How does a nurturing and supportive self-talk differ from rational self-talk?

We may think we are using a self-talk that is supportive, when in fact we are making statements that are merely logical or rational. For example, when panicking we might ask ourselves, *What if I faint?* A rational counterstatement would be, *This is a panic attack. I'm not going to faint. I'll be fine!* When trying to be rational, we might even take it a step further and try to see ourselves as relaxed and feeling confident as we enter the freeway, the mall, or the corner grocery store. Our approach is positive, but not always convincing. That's not to say that rational self-talk doesn't work, only that it's not necessarily effective in every situation. We might have a difficult time believing that we are going to be fine when our panic is already escalating.

A supportive self-talk when panicking would be, *I'm having a panic attack. Just try to go with the feeling.* I found words like *allow* or *float*, or phrases like *Don't fight it* or *Embrace the fear,* to be helpful. While I needed the rational self-talk telling me that nothing was going to happen (other than the panic) and the gentle reassurance that I would be okay, I found it more helpful in the long run to use a self-talk that supported how I was feeling, one that accepted my anxiety symptoms.

How can I learn a more nurturing, supportive self-talk?
First we must listen to the messages we are giving ourselves. Do they support how we are feeling? Are we allowing our anxiety symptoms? Or are we telling ourselves that we have to stop being so anxious? Learning a new way of talking to ourselves takes time.

As we become more aware of our self-talk we might hear ourselves saying, *This is ridiculous! I have to get over this!* or *I must be crazy!* Such remarks are harsh and critical. Their message is: This is not okay. Something is wrong with me and I have to fix it! I have to get rid of this anxiety. Supportive counterstatements would be helpful here. For example, *It's okay for me to be anxious. I am not crazy. The more I can allow my anxiety without fighting it, the better. Trying hard to fix it or get rid of it only makes it worse.*

Permissive self-talk doesn't mean that we're not going to do something about our problem. It only means that we're going to stop tightening the reins, that we are going to step back and allow the anxiety to do what it wants, rather than build up a resistance. In fact, learning a nurturing and supportive self-talk is a good way to start doing something about our anxiety problem.

What do I do when supportive self-talk doesn't work?
Even when we have learned a supportive inner dialogue, there will be days when a critical, nonpermissive self-talk takes over, days when it is difficult to be accepting of our anxiety or panic attacks. At times like this, it is easy to get discouraged and perhaps give up. But we need to remind ourselves that some days the dialogue will work and other days it won't. Despite periodic setbacks, learning a gentle and compassionate inner voice is well worth the time and patience involved.

In the following story, Donna struggles with feelings of failure. Unable to come up with a helpful and supportive self-talk, she discovers a way to work through her feelings until a more gentle self-talk returns.

Donna's Story
There are days when my gentle and compassionate self-talk

is silent, when feelings of failure can bring my spirits down and haunt me. I find myself reliving the sinking feeling of some human error. Past mistakes come back in droves, as if to say, "You've failed again!" No matter how hard I try to console myself, I am bombarded with a harsh and unforgiving self-talk.

Rather than fight it, I simply listen to it as a necessary part of the process of working through my feelings. Finally, when I am willing to let go of my critical self-talk, I try to put things into their proper perspective again. I have discovered that no matter how badly I feel about myself, the feeling will pass and I will be able to rely on a gentle and compassionate self-talk once again.

What if those around me are not supportive?

Even when we learn a supportive self-talk we may still be faced with the harsh comments and criticism of those around us. Referring to friends and family, I often hear Open Door members say, "They just don't get it!" The fact of the matter is, they really *don't* get it. It is difficult for someone who has never experienced a panic attack or suffered from intense anxiety to understand what we are dealing with. In their attempts to be helpful, they tell us, "There's nothing to be afraid of!" "Don't think about it!" "Just do it!"

It is especially difficult when a family member or significant other doesn't take the time to learn about our anxiety problem. People have commented, "I leave books and articles on anxiety and panic attacks lying around the house, but no one bothers to read them." The message we take from this? *It's all in your head* or *I don't have time for this* or *It's your problem, not mine!* This insensitivity, or lack of compassion, makes us feel even more isolated. It is difficult to have lowered expectations of ourselves, to be accepting of our anxiety, and use a supportive self-talk when we are surrounded by apathy. Lack of understanding or indifference not only add to our isolation, but increase our shame.

What about positive affirmations?
If affirmations work, than by all means let's use them. We can write them down on paper and put them on our refrigerator door, on the dash of our car, or in the desk drawer at work. Affirmations can be effective, but for those of us with an anxiety disorder it is important that they be both realistic and believable. For example, if I wake up in the morning and tell myself that *every day in every way I'm feeling better and better*, when, in fact, I am getting out of bed and feeling worse, I'm going to be very discouraged and wonder why the affirmation is not working. It's not working because it's not believable.

The following affirmations, which are a part of the Open Door Program, have been helpful to many anxiety sufferers.[22]

I am learning that my anxiety and panic attacks are manageable
and that I can still function in spite of them

22 Bemis, Judith and Amr Barrada. *Cards for Releasing Fear & Anxiety.* Center City: Haxelden Foundation, 1995.

When nothing seems to help my anxiety, it's important to be okay with that and give myself permission to muddle through the best I can

It helps when I allow the sensations of anxiety or panic— just let them happen without resistance

It helps if I remind myself that this is only a panic attack and that I am not in any physical danger

I will try to lower my expectations and allow for any discomfort that I might experience

Even if I'm not there yet, I will eventually see light at the end of the tunnel

My anxiety or panic attacks are not dangerous. I will be okay

The more permissive I am of my panic feelings, the less frightening they become and the more confidence I gain in working through them

There are times when I'm able to accept my anxiety and times when I'm not. It will help if I try to be accepting of that

It helps if I remind myself that the recovery process is never smooth and that in spite of a setback, I am still making progress

What can I do about anticipatory anxiety?

Anticipatory anxiety is one of the many problems we deal with. Just thinking about going somewhere where we might panic causes a great deal of anxiety. We might spend weeks worrying about a planned event, even obsessing over it. Rather than making dinner reservations, or purchasing theater tickets ahead of time, we would rather do things on the spur of the moment and avoid all the worrying. However, spontaneity isn't always possible. When planning, it might help to give ourselves permission to change our mind at the last minute. By giving ourselves this option, we stand a better chance of following through on our plans. This is illustrated in the following story.

Carol's Story

My husband and I planned to take our daughters to the Children's Theater. Just the thought of ordering tickets raised my anxiety. Once I made the call I knew what would happen: I would worry about being anxious on the day of the performance. It was so discouraging to think that I would always react this way. The "what ifs" were ruthless. *What if I can't go at the last minute and I let my family down? What if I panic on the way there and we have to turn around? What if I panic in the theater and embarrass my family?* I really wasn't sure it was worth all the anxiety the planning caused me.

I decided that the only way I could find peace was to give myself an out. If necessary, I would tell my family that I couldn't go. After all, they wouldn't have to change *their* plans.

On the day of the performance, I took the risk of joining my family, allowing for any discomfort the day might bring. I can't say that I was comfortable the entire time I was at the theater. But having given myself options, I hadn't spent two weeks working myself into a state of nervous exhaustion about the upcoming event.

No matter how many panic attacks I've had, what if this time it isn't panic?

It's okay to ask *What if?* We are not being irrational when we question our symptoms, since they usually resemble a physical problem. For example, we're more likely to associate heart palpitations and shortness of breath with a serious medical issue. I remember asking myself the same question each time I had a panic attack. I couldn't convince myself that I wasn't dying.

A speaker at an Open Door seminar said that at one point he believed that if he could work with panic sufferers when they first started having attacks, he could "nip the problem in the bud." However, he learned that in the early stages of an anxiety disorder there is usually little chance of reassuring the person that their problem is emotional. They are convinced they have some physical illness not yet diagnosed.

I weathered many a panic attack before I was ready to accept the fact that my problem wasn't physical. After a week of extensive tests at a university hospital, I checked out, only to admit myself to another hospital because I believed that the doctors had overlooked the real cause of my symptoms. Again, I was told that there was no physical reason for my complaints. But I didn't give up easily. Still convinced that I had a serious medical problem, I checked into a third hospital for further testing. And, of course, the tests proved negative. It was several more years before I was ready to work on the real source of my anxiety—a major step in my recovery.

Shouldn't I try to stop negative thoughts?
"There seems to be so much emphasis in this program on allowing our thoughts," said a newcomer to our group, "even those that trouble us." It's true. Our program does suggest allowing them, that is, *letting go of the need to control them,* since continually fighting troublesome thoughts can add to our anxiety. You may say, "What? I can't do that! I have to stop thinking this way! If I allow these thoughts, my anxiety will only get worse!" Stopping a negative thought and replacing it with one that is positive certainly sounds like the logical thing to do, but it's important to point out that allowing our thoughts doesn't mean that we focus on them or dwell on them.

I am reminded of my meditation class. The instructor explained that we might have some difficulty with intrusive thoughts during our meditation exercises. Rather than trying to stop them, she told us to merely observe them as they passed through our consciousness. Becoming an observer holds true in our situation as well.

Allowing our thoughts simply means not fighting them or becoming overly disturbed by them. It means looking at them objectively and seeing them as nothing more than that—just thoughts

Negative thoughts aren't the only ones that are disturbing to us. Some may seem strange or "abnormal." For example, when we are in a high place and feel the fear of jumping; or we might think of harming someone for no apparent reason. We tell ourselves, *I must be crazy to think this way. This isn't normal!* But in fact, other anxiety sufferers have similar thoughts. We might remind ourselves that there are any number of people without phobias who have strange thoughts and are not overly troubled by them.

Does thought stopping ever work?

A young man attended an Open Door meeting several years ago. As a recovered agoraphobic, he wanted to share his success with the group. He had been living in Manhattan before moving to the Midwest. He told us about his continuous attempts to overcome his panic problem. We all waited to hear the secret to his success. The group hung on to his every word. "One day," he said, "as I was waiting on a street corner, I felt the anxiety start to build and I thought, *What if I panic?* Tired of living this way, I decided to stop the thought about panicking. To my surprise the panic attack never materialized. After that, I was no longer troubled by panic attacks, nor was I concerned about their recurrence."

We all looked at each other in disbelief. Could it really have been that simple? Chances are, there was more to the story, but it served as a reminder that different strategies work for different people.

Trying to block out troublesome thoughts may work for some of us. For the rest of us, *Just don't think about it!* is not that easy. The more we try not to think about something the more it haunts us. Like a panic attack, the best thing many of us can do is not fight it, and to look at it for what it is, *a thought.*

How can I stop worrying about everything?

Because we see worry as something negative or abnormal, we tell ourselves that we have to stop worrying. We worry about worrying. This is especially true when those around us seem unaffected by the events that cause us so much concern. Like anxiety itself, we see worry as something we need to get rid of. Yet worry can serve a purpose: it can motivate us to do something about what we're worried about, for example, not getting our bills paid on time.

However, many anxiety sufferers worry in order to have some control in their lives. They believe they must remain vigilant to prevent some sort of catastrophe. I have often had the feeling that as long as I am worrying about something, nothing bad will happen. This is not uncommon. Consider the story of the fearful flyer who believed that it was her worry about the aircraft's safety that kept it on course and safe. If she stopped worrying, even for a minute, she believed something catastrophic would happen. (I am not the only one, it turns out, who keeps planes from falling out of the sky.)

Like trying to stop a troublesome thought, trying to stop ourselves from worrying only tends to increase the problem. Someone once told me, "Try to see worry as an option." I found that advice helpful. By allowing myself to worry—or not—I no longer felt so trapped in my thoughts.

What about panic attacks that occur during the night?

One of the reasons we believe panic attacks come from out of the blue, rather than being brought on by a particular thought or feeling, is that we sometimes experience panic during the night. I woke up many times in the throes of a panic attack. Not quite awake and feeling disoriented, I would try to fight the mounting symptoms. I would then reach for the phone to dial 911. I too wondered how I could possibly panic when I was asleep and my body was relaxed. The answer is that the body is relaxed but the mind is not. We take the cares and concerns of the day to bed with us and the mind continues to be occupied with them (evidence of which is dreams).

Rather than fighting the symptoms we need to allow ourselves to have these nocturnal attacks, knowing they are not dangerous, and then try to accept the fact that such episodes are normal. What makes them more terrifying than daytime attacks is that, by the time we're awake and aware of what is happening, the panic has escalated and the best we can do is try to float through it. It might help to focus on one or two words, such as *float* or *allow*.

Points to Remember: *The Gentle Voice Within*

1. There are three different types of self-talk: one that is harsh, critical and nonpermissive; one that is logical or rational; and one that is permissive, gentle and nurturing.

2. A nurturing and supportive self-talk is of prime importance in helping us deal with anxiety and panic attacks. It is gentle and permissive of our thoughts, actions and feelings.

3. We are not being irrational when we question our symptoms. For example, we associate heart palpitations or shortness of breath with medical issues, which is what makes them so frightening.

4. It helps to be aware that there will be days when a critical, nonpermissive self-talk takes over, when it is difficult to be accepting of our anxiety or panic attacks.

5. Affirmations are more helpful for the anxiety or panic sufferer if they are both realistic and believable.

6. We can spend weeks obsessing over a planned activity only to discover that the anticipatory anxiety was worse than the actual event.

7. Strange and "abnormal" thoughts are not uncommon. There are people without an anxiety disorder who have strange thoughts and are not troubled by them.

8. Allowing our thoughts simply means not fighting them or becoming overly disturbed by them. It means looking at our thoughts objectively and seeing them as nothing more than that—just thoughts.

9. We sometimes use worry as a way to control an otherwise uncontrollable situation. We believe that as long as we remain vigilant,

we can ward off catastrophe.

10. Nocturnal panic attacks are not unusual. We take the cares and concerns of the day to bed with us and the mind continues to be occupied with them.

Taking a Closer Look at Our Self-Talk

Where do I usually experience my anxiety or panic attacks? Am I alone or with someone?

1. What is the first thing I say to myself when the attack begins?

2. What might I tell myself to help me get through the situation?

(See suggested answers on page 60.)

How Do We Cope? *At the Grocery Store*

What strategies would you use in the following situation?

You have just arrived at the grocery store. Just as you thought would happen, you feel your heart start to race as you enter the front door. Your first thought is to leave and go back home, but you know from experience that leaving gives you the feeling of having failed. Besides, you need groceries. *(See suggested answers on page 60.)*

More on Self-Talk: *The Gentle Voice Within*

What Am I Really Saying to Myself?

Here are three examples of how we might talk to ourselves at the onset of a panic attack. Example 1 demonstrates a common response to one of our greatest fears, panicking in public and making a fool of ourselves. Example 2 attempts to stay in control by using distraction. Example 3 gives us permission to experience the anxiety or panic, and reminds us to give ourselves the option of staying or leaving.

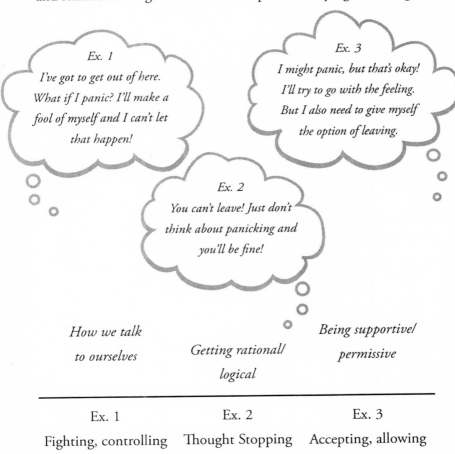

Ex. 1
I've got to get out of here.
What if I panic? I'll make a
fool of myself and I can't let
that happen!

Ex. 3
I might panic, but that's okay!
I'll try to go with the feeling.
But I also need to give myself
the option of leaving.

Ex. 2
You can't leave! Just don't
think about panicking and
you'll be fine!

How we talk
to ourselves

Getting rational/
logical

Being supportive/
permissive

Ex. 1	Ex. 2	Ex. 3
Fighting, controlling	Thought Stopping	Accepting, allowing

(Suggested answers from page 58.)

Taking a Closer Look at Our Self-Talk (question #2)

1. I'm not sure I can do this. Sometimes the best I can do is try.
2. If I'm anxious, I'm anxious. I'll do the best I can under the circumstances.
3. I don't have to do this. I've chosen to take this risk. It will help if I can see it as practice.
4. The more I tell myself I have to do this without being anxious, the more pressure I put on myself.

How Do We Cope? Shopping at the Grocery Store

Strategy A: I can take the risk of going in and giving myself a lot of permission to feel anxious. I can buy one item, all of the groceries on my list, or nothing at all. It helps if I give myself options and see this as practice.

Strategy B: I can practice going through the door, and then I can practice leaving and being okay with that. Sometimes just sitting in the parking lot can be good practice. (This might mean having someone else shop for my groceries.) A supportive and nurturing self-talk is very important at this time.

THIS IS WHO I AM TODAY

With each wave of panic I tried to visualize myself
stepping into it or embracing it

After having a severe panic attack that left me quite shaken, I tried to schedule an appointment with my therapist. Unable to see him because of his busy schedule, it was suggested that I speak to another psychologist at the clinic instead. I was skeptical that anyone could help me on a one-time basis, but I was desperate and made an appointment to see him that same day.

During our session, he suggested that the next time I was anxious I should say to myself, "This is who I am today; I'm "Anxious Judy." At first, I scoffed at the idea and wondered what good that could possibly do. In retrospect, I consider it one of the best pieces of advice anyone ever gave me. Many times over I have repeated the phrase—whether it's Anxious Judy, Tired Judy, Lonely Judy, or Sad Judy—I've simply filled in the blank.

With this suggestion the therapist was telling me to "allow" the feeling, whatever it was, to identify with it, take hold of it and make it mine. By saying, *This is who I am* today! I was putting the feeling into its proper perspective. It was like saying, *This feeling is only temporary; this too shall pass.*

Is allowing anxiety the same as acceptance?

Allowing anxiety and *acceptance* are similar, but there is a difference. Allowing is more of an act of surrender, giving in to our symptoms each time they occur. It is what Claire Weekes refers to as *floating* through the anxiety or panic attack.[23] Acceptance, on the other hand, is more encompassing. For example, even if we allow our symptoms, it doesn't necessarily mean that we're accepting them, nor does it mean that we're accepting the fact that we have an anxiety disorder.

> *Allowing our anxiety symptoms means not fighting them.*
> *It means letting them run their course each time they occur.*
> *Acceptance means embracing our anxiety or panic attacks*
> *(or disorder) without judging ourselves*

How can I possibly allow myself to panic?

Considering the intensity of a panic attack, it does seem next to impossible to just allow the feeling. There's that inner voice desperately telling us: "Do something!" However, when we come to believe that the worst that will happen is intense discomfort, it *is* possible to allow our panic symptoms without being overwhelmed by them. Over a period of time we gain confidence in our own nervous system, confidence in our body. We trust that we will be

---

23 Weekes, Claire. *Hope And Help For Your Nerves.* New York: A Signet Book, 1990. Page 25.

able to handle the panic episode should it occur. What frightens us is the feeling of *helplessness,* the *not knowing* what will happen when we panic *or how long* it will last. For some of us it may help to visualize a ceiling—seeing the panic go just so high and then seeing it come down again—rather than thinking of the panic as unending.

No one wants to allow panic attacks to disrupt their life. When we tell ourselves, *This is who I am* today—that is, allowing ourselves to experience the panic symptoms—we are not minimizing the problem. We all know it is not that easy. No matter how many times we panic, it is a terrifying experience. Feeling out of control and on the verge of emotional or physical danger, it is a natural reaction to try to fight the mounting symptoms every step of the way. But *allowing,* not *fighting,* will keep us from feeling overwhelmed. In the following story, Kelley explains how the word "allow" not only helped her make it to class, but helped her remain.

Kelley's Story

I was told that an artistic outlet might be helpful in alleviating my panic attacks. So I signed up for a dance class. Based on the assumption that more is better, I registered for an acting class as well. I figured that if one class didn't work the other one might. And the two together would be a sure thing. No sooner had I sent in my application than I was already anticipating with the "what ifs." *What if I'm anxious and can't make it to class? What if I get halfway there and have to turn back? What if I have a panic attack during class and have to leave?*

63

When the evening of the first class arrived, what seemed like a good idea several weeks ago, no longer looked promising. However, I gave myself permission to turn the car around at any time and head back home. The symptoms were relentless. But I stayed with the feeling the best I could. I told myself that I had experienced these panicky feelings many times before, especially behind the wheel. So what else was new? By allowing the anxiety, I was able to make it to my class. I sat close to the door and continued to allow the discomfort. My goal was to stay for ten minutes if I could handle it. If not, it was okay to go home. But by the time the ten minutes were up I was so involved in the lesson I didn't feel the need to leave.

I've been told that I should get angry at my panic attacks
Dr. Lynne Freeman, in her book *Panic Free*,[24] suggests getting angry and fighting the panic rather than giving in to it. This is another example of different strategies working for different people.

Before I was diagnosed with panic disorder and realized what was happening to me, I sometimes used this approach. I remember struggling with the panic and getting so angry that I would reach for the vacuum cleaner and clean my carpets with a vengeance. I'm sure I used up a lot of adrenaline in the process. Although it wasn't a cure-all, it gave me temporary relief from the symptoms

---

23 Freeman, Lynne. *Panic Free: Eliminate Anxiety/Panic Attacks Without Drugs And Take Control of Your Life.* New York: Barclay House, 1995. page 78.

and helped me muster the courage to leave the house on those difficult days. For long-term results, however, I discovered that the key was being more accepting of my anxiety and allowing it to run its course without overreacting.

I do well for a while and then my symptoms seem to change

Over a period of time anxiety or panic symptoms can become less frightening. We know from experience that they're not going to cause us to make a fool of ourselves nor harm us. But no sooner do we get used to them when new and unfamiliar ones suddenly appear. It's as though our body has found another way to alarm us. Being aware that this can happen may make the new symptoms less frightening and therefore easier to deal with. When in doubt, however, it is advisable to check with a doctor to make sure that new symptoms are related to stress and not medical (if for no other reason than to put our mind at ease).

Why isn't the word "control" used in this program?

We see book titles telling us to *stop panicking*. We hear speakers talk about *conquering* or *mastering* our fear. The message is the same: we shouldn't be anxious and we must do something about our anxiety problem. The fact is, we're already working hard at *fixing* and *controlling*. But rather than struggling to stay in control, which is a significant part of our problem, our answer lies at the opposite end of the spectrum: let go. It is the *letting go of control* and *allowing ourselves to be anxious* that many of us have found most helpful.

Can I use distraction as a coping strategy?

Distraction is an option, but it's temporary. Distraction also reinforces the belief that being anxious is not okay. We frantically tell ourselves to keep busy or think about something else in order to take our mind off the anxiety or avoid the onset of a panic attack. But a lot of effort is needed to stop a thought or feeling by keeping busy or thinking about something else. It can be a no-win situation. Even when distraction does work, we may find ourselves anticipating the next anxiety or panic episode. But over time, and with acceptance, the symptoms become less frightening. When that happens, we no longer need distraction as a coping strategy.

In the following story, Paul tries to put his mind on something other than his anxiety and finds his symptoms increasing.

Paul's Story

There were many times when I tried distraction as a way of warding off a panic attack, but it didn't always work for me. I remember one day, waiting to make a left-hand turn at a red light. As I sat there, I suddenly felt trapped. I had no choice but to wait for the light to change and sensed the panic building. I reached for the radio dial and frantically searched for a music station that would distract me. At that moment I had the strange feeling that I was running away, which only made my anxiety worse. Before the light turned green, I was in the middle of a full-blown panic attack.

How is "being involved" different from distraction?

Distraction means counting backwards from one hundred, memorizing license plates, or similar activities. Being involved means taking part in a conversation, watching a video, or reading a book. Like distraction, being involved and focusing on anything outside of our anxiety is not easy. Unlike distraction, we don't do it to *get rid of* our anxiety or block it out. We don't approach it thinking that if we put our mind on something else, the anxiety will go away. Instead, we take our anxiety with us—aware of how we are feeling and allowing our symptoms—as we get involved in the activity at hand. In doing so, we might want to remind ourselves, *This is who I am today.*

Points to Remember: *This is Who I Am Today*

1. "This is who I am *today*" is like saying "This is only temporary," or "This too shall pass."

2. *Allowing* our anxiety symptoms means not fighting them. It means letting them run their course each time they occur.

3. It is the feeling of helplessness that frightens us—not knowing what will happen when we panic or how long it will last.

4. Visualizing a ceiling can help reassure us that the panic attacks will only go so far and then diminish again.

5. Our anxiety symptoms can change. It's as though our body is trying to find a new way to alarm us.

6. Not only is distraction temporary, but it reinforces the belief that it's not okay to be anxious.

7. Like distraction, becoming involved and focusing on anything

outside of our anxiety is not easy. Unlike distraction, getting involved isn't something we do to get rid of or block out our anxiety. We simply take our anxiety with us.

8. Over a period of time we gain confidence in our own nervous system, confidence in our body. We trust that we will be able to handle the anxiety.

Taking a Closer Look at Our Self-Talk

If you have experienced any recent changes in your symptoms, what was your reaction?

1. How might your self-talk have helped you in this situation?
2. What else might you have said to put your mind at ease, so you could be more accepting of these changes? *(See suggested answers on page 70.)*

How Do We Cope? *At the Theater*

What coping strategies would you use in the following situation?

You have just arrived at the movie theater with friends. They want to sit up front, preferably in the center. You know this will be difficult for you, but you are too embarrassed to say anything.

(See suggested answers on page 70.)

More on Self-Talk: *This is Who I am Today*
What Am I Really Saying to Myself?
Here are three examples of how we might talk to ourselves at the onset of a panic attack or when we are feeling anxious. Example 1 demonstrates a need to stay in control. Example 2 attempts to block out the anxiety symptoms by distraction. Example 3 allows the anxiety or panic without trying to control it.

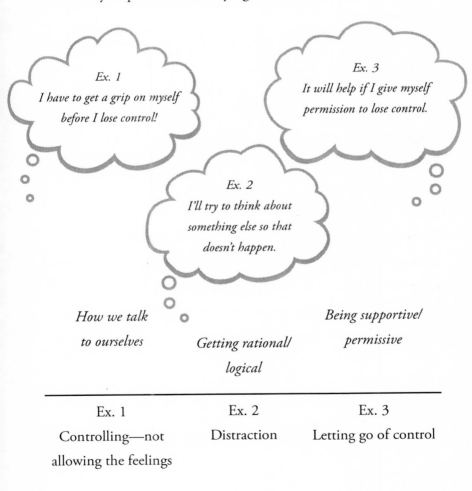

Ex. 1
I have to get a grip on myself before I lose control!

Ex. 3
It will help if I give myself permission to lose control.

Ex. 2
I'll try to think about something else so that doesn't happen.

How we talk to ourselves

Getting rational/ logical

Being supportive/ permissive

Ex. 1	Ex. 2	Ex. 3
Controlling—not allowing the feelings	Distraction	Letting go of control

(Suggested answers for page 68.)

Taking a Closer Look at Our Self-Talk (question #2)

1. The less I resist these anxiety symptoms, the better.

2. I've had this feeling before and I'll probably have it again. I'll just try to let it happen.

3. The worst that will happen is that I'll feel anxious. I don't have to do anything to fix it.

4. This is scary, but I'll try to go with the feeling. The worst part of this is feeling afraid.

How Do We Cope? At the Theater

Strategy A: I can sit with them and tough it out, allowing the feelings of anxiety that occur in situations such as this. I have the choice of telling them or not telling them how I am feeling.

Strategy B: I can explain to them that I have a difficult time sitting up front and in the center of the row. They can sit where they choose, but I'm going to sit further back. It will help if I give myself lots of permission to do this and then feel okay about it.

SLOWING DOWN IN A FAST-PACED WORLD

My therapist handed me a piece of paper. On it he had written,
"Slow down." It was the beginning of my recovery

S lowing down can make a significant difference in our anxiety
level. It can give us a feeling of being more centered, more in
tune to what is going on around us. Light-headedness, dizziness, or
feeling off-balance are symptoms of rushing. However, the idea of
slowing down seems to go against everything our society dictates.
The message we get is, the faster you work, the more efficient you
are. In today's workplace it is not unusual to see a decrease in staff
and an increase in workload. As job responsibilities grow and pressure builds, our stress level increases.

We seem willing to fill up a 16-hour day. Many of us have, or
have had, full-time jobs, families, household responsibilities and
social commitments. As if that weren't enough, we take on other
activities out of interest, social pressure, or the inability to say no.
Of course, we expect ourselves to handle them all with maximum
efficiency. Unfortunately, little time is left for recreation, relaxation,
or taking care of our physical and emotional needs. We constantly
need to be busy. What we don't realize is how our numerous

commitments and high expectations are taking their toll.

What can I do to help myself slow down?

The obvious answer, of course, is to take on fewer activities in a day and allow ourselves more leisure time. Sounds easy, but we all know it's not.

Slowing down is a difficult task, especially when working under a heavy schedule, which is often the case. Feeling overwhelmed with the day's activities, our mind tends to race to the next project before we even get to it. At this point, we might consider making a list and prioritizing it. Lists, however, can also create a problem if we expect to get everything done in short order. What helps is to be satisfied crossing off only one or two items rather than finishing the whole list by the end of the day.

As difficult as it might be, we need to take time away from the desk, the telephone, and the usual everyday demands. However, like a harsh and critical self-talk, for many of us, *being busy has become a part of who we are.* But with patience and practice we can eventually incorporate slowing down as part of our lifestyle. The following example shows how I dealt with my inherent need to take life at a fast pace.

Judy's Story

As difficult as it was, eventually I reached a point in my recovery when I was able to take life at a slower pace. What I found helpful was to focus on the everyday things I did—

how fast I got dressed in the morning, how fast I put on my makeup, or how fast I ate my breakfast. If I found myself rushing I would stop what I was doing, take a deep breath, and think *heavy*. I let my arms hang loose and allowed gravity to take over. I visualized my feet sinking into the floor and got a feeling of being anchored. I then continued what I had started out to do, only now in slow motion.

What helps me these days when I'm feeling rushed is to focus on the present. I ask myself, *What am I doing right now?* I answer with the fact: *driving a car, organizing a desk drawer.* I then remind myself, *This is all I need to do at this moment. I can handle this.*

A colleague once remarked that she always knew it was me coming down the hall because I walked so fast. I often wondered what she thought after I stopped rushing past her door. For me, not rushing felt like a loss of identity. I missed that person who rushed around getting so much accomplished. It took a while before I got used to the new me. But I discovered that slowing down helped me feel more centered without affecting my productivity.

What about those days when I just can't *slow down?*
There will be days when slowing down seems impossible, just as there are days when it is difficult to maintain a supportive and nurturing self-talk, or be accepting of our anxiety or panic attacks. Whether on the job or at home, we can feel overwhelmed with the

work piling up, countless interruptions, and imposed deadlines. It is times like this when *acceptance* once again becomes a key word. It will help if we can be accepting of our situation, aware that our fast pace might result in an increased level of anxiety. Thus, our self-talk might be: *Of course I'm feeling anxious. My work is very demanding,* or *Why wouldn't I be anxious? This project (work) has to be finished by Friday and I'm really under a lot of pressure.*

Whatever our reason for maintaining a busy lifestyle, it will help if we see ourselves as having options about *how much* we do on any given day. We might remind ourselves that it is still our choice to work at a particular job, take on extra projects, or keep a spotless house. We need to feel that we are in charge; that we can make adjustments in our schedule when necessary. By giving ourselves options, we no longer have to feel trapped in an endless cycle of activity.

Does slowing down mean I have to stop what I'm doing?
We don't necessarily have to stop what we're doing, such as quitting our job or giving up our hobbies or social activities. We like being busy. It gives us focus, structure and purpose. The question is, are we keeping busy because we want to be busy or because we want to take our mind off our anxiety or that next panic attack? As a diversion, constantly keeping busy only tends to make us more anxious. It can be an exercise in futility (not to mention exhausting). There's nothing wrong with being busy, but we need balance in our lives. We need to take time for fun and relaxation.

But even with a busy schedule, we can approach our tasks in a way that is not so rushed. This will involve lowering our expectations, taking out time limits whenever possible, and staying in the present by focusing on the task at hand. It will mean taking breaks throughout the day and even allowing ourselves time to do nothing.

But if I don't hurry, I'll panic!

We sometimes *think* that if we rush through a feared situation there will be less chance to be anxious or have a panic attack. However, rushing doesn't ward off symptoms. What is helpful, at any pace, is to allow the anxiety to run its course. By doing so, *regardless of where we are*, we discover that we no longer have to run away from it. In the following story, Mara finds that it's easier to shop when she slows down and allows her anxiety symptoms.

Mara's Story

I remember standing at the entrance to the grocery store, anticipating the anxiety I was sure I'd have as soon as I stepped through the door. While mustering up my courage, I visualized the locations of the items I needed. I then went directly to the shelves, quickly gathered up my groceries, and headed for the checkout counter. With any luck there wouldn't be a line. I had rushed through stores on many occasions seeking to get outside before the panicky feelings hit.

What a surprise I got when I discovered that slowing down and allowing the panic actually made it easier for me to stay in the store and finish my shopping. As I became more accepting of the anxiety symptoms, I discovered that I was no longer afraid of them, and they became less and less of a problem.

Why are weekends so difficult?

Even when there isn't an increase in workload or deadlines to meet, we can still feel anxious. This is especially frustrating. Weekends, for example, can be difficult. Having more time to focus on our anxiety, we look forward to Monday morning when we can get back to our usual routine. Being very busy becomes comfortable for us, while having too much time on our hands can be a pretty scary prospect.

Perhaps part of the problem is the sudden change of pace on weekends. It's like getting off of a roller coaster and feeling like we're still moving. It could be the expectation that, since it is our day off, we *should* feel relaxed. Or maybe we feel overwhelmed with a list of chores that didn't get done during the week. Whatever the reason, it is especially difficult to be accepting of that rushed feeling and the anxiety that accompanies it on days when most people are taking time to relax and enjoy themselves.

We can make our weekends more manageable by understanding why they're a problem. If we have high expectations, that is, if we expect to be relaxed, we need to lower them and allow for any anxiety we might have. If we're overwhelmed by a list of chores, we need to prioritize them. Even allow some of them to slide. As for other people relaxing and enjoying the weekend, well, it's not necessarily true.

Points to Remember: *Slowing Down*

1. Slowing down can make a significant difference in our anxiety level. It can help to alleviate such symptoms as light-headedness, dizziness, or feeling off-balance.

2. Not only do we have a tendency to take on more than we can handle, we think we should be able to perform all tasks with maximum efficiency.

3. Making a list and prioritizing it can be helpful as long as we don't put it into a time-frame with high expectations of getting everything done.

4. By giving ourselves options about how much to take on, we no longer have to feel trapped in an endless cycle of activity.

5. On days when we can't slow down it will help to be accepting of an increased level of anxiety.

6. When we give ourselves permission to experience the anxiety or panic, regardless of where we are, we discover that we no longer have to run away from it.

7. Constantly keeping busy as a diversion, that is, rushing around to take our mind off of our anxiety, only tends to make matters worse.

8. We can still feel rushed even when we don't have an increased workload or deadlines to meet.

Taking a Closer Look at Our Self-Talk

When or where do I usually find myself rushing?

1. What strategies might I use to help me to slow down?

2. How might my self-talk help me when I'm feeling rushed? *(See suggested answers on page 80.)*

How Do We Cope? *Feeling Rushed*

What coping strategies would you use in the following situation?

You have a dinner engagement with a friend. Reservations are for 7:00 p.m. Since you don't get home from work until 6:00 you don't have much time to get ready. You know that in order to be there on time you will have to hurry, and as a result you might experience a lot of anxiety. *(See suggested answers on page 80.)*

More on Self-Talk: *Slowing Down*

What Am I Really Saying to Myself?

Here are three examples of how we might talk to ourselves when we are having a difficult time slowing down. Example 1 demonstrates the frustration of experiencing the symptoms that result from speeding up. Example 2 gives a simple explanation for the symptoms. Example 3 uses a gentler voice. It replaces "should" with "it would help if." It also encourages us to allow the dizziness caused by rushing.

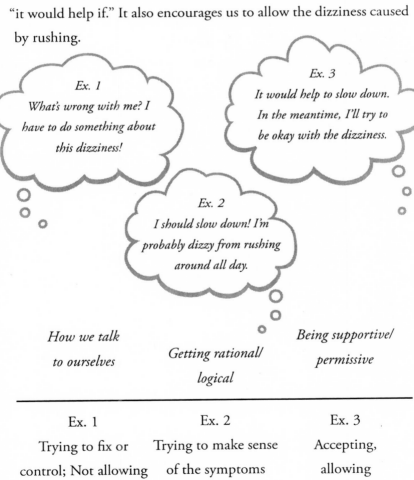

Ex. 1
What's wrong with me? I have to do something about this dizziness!

Ex. 3
It would help to slow down. In the meantime, I'll try to be okay with the dizziness.

Ex. 2
I should slow down! I'm probably dizzy from rushing around all day.

How we talk to ourselves

Getting rational/ logical

Being supportive/ permissive

Ex. 1	Ex. 2	Ex. 3
Trying to fix or control; Not allowing	Trying to make sense of the symptoms	Accepting, allowing

(Suggested answers for page 78.)

Taking a Closer Look at Our Self-Talk (question #2)

1. I'm running late. It will help if I give myself permission not to be on time so that I won't have to rush.
2. It will help to slow everything down and focus on the moment. I can handle what I'm doing right now.
3. I feel I'm not getting as much accomplished now that I've slowed down. The best I can do is accept that.
4. I just can't seem to slow down today. It will help if I allow myself to feel rushed, even if it means being anxious.

How Do We Cope? Feeling Rushed

Strategy A: I can arrange to leave work a few minutes early. If not, I can try to deal with the time-crunch by giving myself permission to experience the anxiety that comes with rushing.

Strategy B: If I find that I can't make it by 7:00 p.m., I can call my friend and explain that I'll be late. This may be difficult, since I like to be on time. A gentle self-talk will help.

LOWERED EXPECTATIONS:
A POSITIVE APPROACH

Throughout the day I kept lowering my expectations.
Taking it one step at a time, I told myself, It's okay to be anxious!

At an Open Door meeting one night, we discussed two important topics: acceptance and keeping expectations low. Each person at the meeting, though dealing with a different issue or feared situation, felt that these two strategies made a marked difference in how they dealt with their anxiety and their progress in their recovery.

"I now see my anxiety as my friend," said one member of the group. "I just tell myself, here's my friend again. It's okay." Another remarked, "While traveling, I will probably be anxious and I can accept that. When you think about it, that's the worst that will happen. It helps if I keep my expectations low." A member who was anticipating a flight noted, "Isn't it amazing how lowering our expectations can really make a difference?"

There's often an element of surprise at how well we do when we lower our expectations and give ourselves permission to be anxious. As we see the difference it makes in our anxiety level, we come to realize what an important role it plays in our recovery.

Low Expectations? Sounds negative to me!

Having low expectations might sound negative, but it can take off the added pressure of having to perform anxiety-free. It is one of the many paradoxes in the recovery process. When we set our expectations too high, that is, when we don't give ourselves permission to be anxious, we build up resistance. We put all our energy into controlling our symptoms, which only increases our anxiety. Here is an example. We might say to ourselves, *I want to meet my friend at the mall today, but what if I'm anxious? I just can't let that happen!* A more helpful self-talk would be, *I want to meet my friend at the mall today. I might feel anxious, and even have a panic attack, but it will help if I can allow that to happen.* With a permissive self-talk, we stand a better chance of making it to the mall.

Lowering our expectations and allowing for discomfort is a powerful strategy. To be clear, we are not saying, *I'm going to have a terrible time when I go out today!* We are not giving ourselves a negative message. We are simply saying, *I just might be anxious when I go out and that's okay!* We allow the possibility of experiencing anxiety. There is no feeling of doomsday in the latter statement, just one of acceptance and lowered expectations.

Low expectations means allowing for any anxiety or panic we might experience rather than expecting to perform anxiety-free

How can I possibly think in terms of lowering my expectations?

It seems contrary.

Not everyone agrees with the concept of lowering expectations. When facing a feared situation, some experts say that we should change our perception and see ourselves as "brave." I think this idea falls into the same category as "Pull yourself up by your boot straps." When we are consumed by fear, it is difficult to see ourselves as brave. And if we are unable to do so, we may feel shame.

In my own experience with agoraphobia, it was a long time before I could lower my expectations and allow my panic attacks. Before learning this important strategy, it only seemed logical that I try to control my anxiety with high expectations, positive affirmations and distraction. But the symptoms were intense and at times overwhelming, making it difficult to focus on anything outside them. However, with time and practice I was able to use this effective strategy.

Wouldn't the thought of panicking create more of a problem?

It does seem logical that the more we raise our expectations and not think about panicking, the more successful we would be in preventing a panic reaction. Here again lies a paradox. The reality is that most of us are already trying hard to stop the thought of panicking. We try even harder to conjure up a positive image of ourselves as relaxed and confident. But we soon discover that trying not to think about the panic doesn't always work in our favor, and often leaves us feeling as though we have failed. So what do we do? We can begin by lowering our expectations and allowing for the possibility of panicking.

I feel like I'm setting myself up for failure by not focusing on
  a more positive outcome

If it works to focus on a positive outcome, such as visualizing ourselves entering a feared situation anxiety-free, then by all means let's do it. But many of us have tried this positive approach time and time again and it hasn't worked. Frustrated and discouraged, we feel we have failed at something that shouldn't be all that difficult. After all, positive thinking results in a positive outcome—or so we've been told. Unfortunately, this result doesn't always hold true for those of us with an anxiety disorder.

By giving ourselves permission to be anxious, we're not setting ourselves up for a bad day. We're simply allowing for whatever happens—even if it means having a less than perfect outcome. Living in a world of high expectations, where we're taught to think positively or aim high, the idea of having low expectations becomes a confusing concept. Even when we understand its effectiveness, it is a difficult theory to explain to family, friends, or colleagues. Perhaps we simply need to tell them that by lowering our expectations and allowing our anxiety we're putting less pressure on ourselves and are therefore less anxious. In the following story, it was low expectations that helped Bonnie stay through the concert.

Bonnie's Story

A friend and I were attending a concert. Although it had been some time since my last panic attack, I was under a great deal of stress and my anxiety level was higher than usual. Our seats were located sixth row center. Leaving would definitely attract the attention of both audience and performer. As we waited for the concert to begin, I looked around for the exits. I wasn't planning to leave, but it helped to know that I had that option.

The music started and my anxiety increased. I felt my heart pounding from the rush of adrenaline. First thought: *What if I pass out?* Response: *That's not going to happen and if it does, I'm with someone who will help me.* Second thought: *I will cause a disturbance and people will be upset with me.* Response: *People are more compassionate than that. They will want to help me.* Supportive thought: *Embrace the fear. Try not to fight it. Just go with the feeling.*

My anxiety persisted, but I kept lowering my expectations and floated through the disturbing sensations the best I could. By the end of the first piece, my anxiety level had dropped considerably—thanks to my self-talk.

What about positive thinking?

If anyone knows the power of the mind, it's those of us who experience anxiety and panic attacks. For example, we know just how far we can go before panicking—whether it's one block or two, the first floor or the second. We can imagine the worst that could possibly happen to us if we were to go one step further. This could be seen as negative thinking resulting in a negative outcome. Realizing this, it seems only logical that we turn our thinking around and make the mind work for us in a more positive way. For example, if I tell myself I *can* walk more than two blocks or climb more than two flights of stairs I should be able to do just that. It's only a case of mind over matter. When that doesn't happen, we may tell ourselves, *Not only am I anxious, but I'm a negative thinker as well.* This results in more shame.

The key point here is *logic*. Why would logic work when there's nothing logical about anxiety or panic attacks? If all we had to do was to think positively, we wouldn't have this problem. I believe in the power of positive thinking. But those of us with an anxiety disorder are usually too frightened about what is happening to us to use it as a coping strategy. "Allow" is still the magic word. And allowing or lowering our expectations come with *acceptance*.

Points to Remember: *Low Expectations*

1. Keeping our expectations low means allowing for any anxiety or panic that we might experience, rather than expecting ourselves to perform anxiety-free.
2. When we have high expectations, we build up resistance. We put all of our energy into trying to control our symptoms.
3. For the true anxiety or panic sufferer, positive thinking does not necessarily result in positive outcomes.

4. Rather than trying not to think about panicking, it works better to simply answer the question, What if I panic? Answering What if? questions can help us plan ways to deal with difficult situations.

5. By giving ourselves permission to be anxious, we're not setting ourselves up for a bad day. We're simply allowing for whatever happens—even if it means having a less than perfect outcome.

6. Lowering our expectations and allowing for discomfort is a powerful strategy.

Taking a Closer Look at Our Self-Talk

When approaching a difficult situation, what are my expectations?

1. Do I allow for any discomfort or do I tell myself I should be able to perform with little or no anxiety?

2. What might I say to myself that will allow me to be anxious?

(See suggested answers on page 89.)

How Do We Cope? *Anticipating an Upcoming Event*

What coping strategies would you use in the following situation?

You have just ordered tickets for a play that your family has been looking forward to seeing. You have two weeks until the event. You're concerned that you might not be able to go because of your anxiety or panic attacks. You would feel guilty if you decided not to go because you think that would spoil everyone's fun. *(See suggested answers on page 89.)*

More on Self-Talk: *Low Expectations*

What Am I Really Saying to Myself?

Here are three examples of how we might talk to ourselves when experiencing anxiety or panic attacks. Example 1 demonstrates how we usually talk to ourselves. Example 2 demonstrates how our expectations can go up when we have had previous success in a place where we usually feel anxious. Example 3 gives us permission to experience the anxiety regardless of the circumstances.

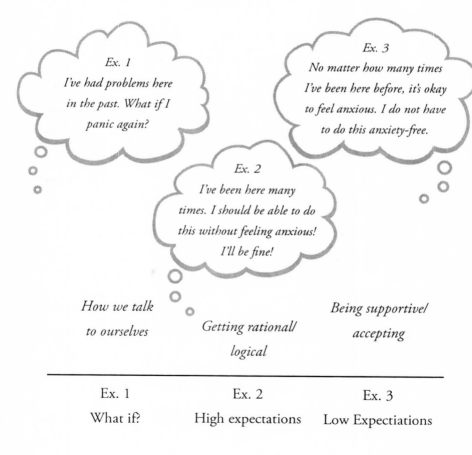

Ex. 1
I've had problems here in the past. What if I panic again?

Ex. 3
No matter how many times I've been here before, it's okay to feel anxious. I do not have to do this anxiety-free.

Ex. 2
I've been here many times. I should be able to do this without feeling anxious! I'll be fine!

How we talk to ourselves

Getting rational/ logical

Being supportive/ accepting

Ex. 1	Ex. 2	Ex. 3
What if?	High expectations	Low Expectiations

(Suggested answers for page 87.)

Taking a Closer Look at Our Self-Talk (question #2)

1. I might have a difficult time when I go out today, but that's okay.
2. The more I can allow myself not to do well, the better.
3. It will help if I lower my expectations and allow for whatever happens. It's okay to be anxious.
4. Why wouldn't I feel this way? This is how I sometimes respond to stressful situations.

How Do We Cope? Anticipating an Upcoming Event

Strategy A: I can give myself an out. If I can't go at the last minute I can tell my family or friends to go without me. They can still have a good time. The challenge will be feeling okay about that decision.

Strategy B: I can visualize the worst scenario and mentally work my way through it. In other words, I can develop a plan for dealing with my worst fears.

FEELING THE FEAR AND TAKING THE RISK

Taking risks means going into the places we fear.
It means allowing for any discomfort we might experience

Claire Weekes writes about a door marked "Utter Acceptance." She says that peace lies on the other side.[25] In other words, we must be willing to go through the door of complete acceptance in order to find recovery. To do so, we need to trust that we can make it to the other side in spite of our weak knees, heart palpitations, and sense of impending doom. By taking risks, we expand our boundaries; whereas, the more we fall into a pattern of avoidance, the more difficult it is to go into the places we fear.

You might be thinking, *I am taking risks, but I'm still white-knuckling my way through feared situations.* This is what I thought until I learned a more supportive self-talk, one that not only accepted my anxiety, but also removed the possibility of failure if I had difficulty coping. This brings us to an important paradox in our program: taking risks, but at the same time giving ourselves permission to leave if we feel overwhelmed.

---

25 Weekes, *Simple, Effective Treatment of Agoraphobia,* pages 111-114.

But isn't leaving a feared situation a form of avoidance?

It can be. It all depends on the message we give ourselves about leaving. Staying in a feared situation when we are anxious or panicking sounds logical, since it's the avoidance that appears to be the problem. Yet this program gives us the option to leave at any time. Since leaving is considered avoiding, it may seem we're being given a double message. The question, however, isn't whether we stay or leave, but what we say to ourselves as we do so.

Let's say we're at a social gathering and having anxiety symptoms that just won't let up. As we look around the room and see everyone having a good time, we wonder, *What is wrong with me? Why am I having this problem? No one else here is feeling this way. This isn't normal! What if it gets worse?* Notice that with all our comparing and catastrophizing we haven't given ourselves permission to experience our anxiety. We feel progressively worse until we just can't take it anymore and decide to leave. We discreetly slip out the door, hoping no one will notice.

What happens next is all too familiar. Our self-talk shames us for being unable to tough it out: *I've failed again. I just don't have what it takes to deal with this!* Considering our harsh and demeaning inner dialogue, it was a no-win situation whether we stayed or left. Our feelings of failure and subsequent shame will make it that much more difficult to take that risk again.

Now let's take that same scenario and introduce a different kind of self-talk. This time, as we look around at the other guests, we choose not to compare ourselves to them. Instead, we might say, *I'm really feeling anxious tonight. So what else is new? It will help if I allow these feelings rather than fight them or try to fix them. Nothing is going to happen to me other than feeling very uncomfortable.* We might even consider this a good opportunity to practice being anxious.

Giving ourselves permission to leave at any time can help to alleviate the feeling of being trapped. For example, *It's okay for me to leave. I haven't failed in any way. It helps to give myself choices.* Knowing we have that option, without seeing it as failure, can actually increase our chances of staying. However, if we should decide to leave, we do so with no shame attached.

We reassure ourselves that leaving is also good practice. We might even give ourselves credit for staying as long as we did, even if it was for a short period of time. Not seeing this as a failure will make it easier for us to return to a similar situation in the future. As we can see, it didn't matter whether we stayed or left. Our inner dialogue was nurturing and supportive, and with either decision we felt good about ourselves.

Staying in an uncomfortable situation can give us confidence that we can still function in spite of our anxiety. We need to know that we can cope when necessary. However, if our self-talk is constantly giving us negative feedback while we're in that situation, we haven't gained much. As an agoraphobic, I repeatedly white-knuckled my way through places where I thought I might panic. But until I learned a more nurturing and permissive way of talking to myself, I merely kept my panic attacks at bay.

In the following story, Rick discovers what a difference it can make when we give ourselves options.

Rick's Story

The other day I went to get my hair cut. As I sat down in the chair I started thinking about what it used to be like when I went to the barber shop. Just the thought of going increased my anxiety. Only on good days was it possible to get a hair cut, and at its best, it was a white-knuckle experience. I had visions of going to work the next day with only half of my hair cut and trying to explain my new hairstyle. Looking back, I can see the tremendous pressure I was putting on myself. *I have to control myself! I can't be anxious! I can't leave!* More than once I couldn't even go into the shop.

Now when I sit in that chair, I tell myself I can leave at any time and that's fine. I can come back whenever I want to. If I need to I can tell the barber that I get anxious at times like this. I've done this once or twice, and everyone has said, "No problem. If you need to leave you can come back later today."

It's important for me to give myself permission to be anxious because that's part of who I am. At times, I still feel anxious while sitting there, but so what? This is true for my trips to the dentist and doctor as well. What has changed is my attitude toward my anxiety. It has taken lots of practice and lots of allowing for whatever happens. Because I can accept whatever happens, my anxiety is just not that big of a deal anymore.

Why does it seem easier to take risks on some days more than others?
One of our many frustrations is that our anxiety symptoms are not consistent. For example, one day we might notice little or no anxiety while shopping, whereas the next day it's there to greet us as we approach the entrance to the mall. This inconsistency or un-predictability leaves us wondering what to expect each time we go shopping, get in the car to drive across town, or eat at our favorite restaurant. But we need to be okay with this variability and accept it as part of the overall problem. Acceptance and low expectations continue to be important strategies for taking risks.

It is difficult enough to take risks on good days. When we are feeling anxious, it's much harder. I once remarked to a friend, "I would take more risks if I just felt good." When you think about it, how many people feel like going out and doing anything when they don't feel well? It is understandable, then, that we hesitate to venture out on days when we are feeling especially sensitized. Doing so will take a self-talk that is both supportive and nurturing.

What can I do on days when nothing seems to work?
Muddle. Put one foot in front of the other and just make it through the day. When nothing we do seems to be working, we need to con-tinue to allow our anxiety symptoms rather than insist on comfort. A returning group member wanted us to know how well she was

doing now and explained that "it was muddling that got me through those difficult days when nothing else worked."

I'm running out of excuses for not going out with my friends. Now what?
We may become very good at making up excuses for not joining our friends for lunch, a movie, or shopping. While hoping to convince others with our excuses, we are painfully aware of the real reason for avoiding these situations. I remember sending my children off to the beach on several occasions with the neighbors while I stayed in the safety of my home. Finally, one of the moms asked me, "What do you do in the house all day?" How could I tell her that I felt safer at home than I did at the beach? I didn't understand what was happening to me and there was no way I could explain it to her. I decided not to tell her anything about my anxiety. Instead, I simply said, "I've been very busy lately."

Practice makes perfect, but what does "practice" mean for us?
Rather than thinking, *I must go to the grocery store without having any anxiety*, *practice* means going there and *practicing* being anxious. With this permissive self-talk, it doesn't matter what the outcome is because there is no possibility of failure. Claire Weekes originally advanced this concept in her book, *Simple, Effective Treatment of Agoraphobia.*[26] I found it especially helpful. It was easier for me to take risks when I approached a feared situation as practice rather

------

26 Weekes, *Simple, Effective Treatment of Agoraphobia,* page 80.

than worrying about how well I would do.

The issue isn't whether we feel anxious or panicky, it's how we respond to these feelings. If we react with alarm, we only reinforce our symptoms. Claire Weekes reminds us, "Don't be bluffed by physical feelings."[27] I have said that to myself many times. The big "bluff" is that our symptoms fool us into thinking that we are in some kind of danger, that we're going to make a fool of ourselves, die, or go crazy.

I'm afraid to tell anyone about my anxiety or panic attacks

Many of us are hesitant to discuss our anxiety or panic attacks because we are afraid people will not understand what we are dealing with. As long as stigma is associated with mental health issues, we will avoid any exposure to protect ourselves from criticism. Yet being open about our anxiety or panic attacks can take away the fear of being found out.

It is not unusual to hear such comments as, "It's a lot easier now that my family knows about my anxiety problem. I no longer have to hide it," or "I actually feel less anxious in the workplace after telling my boss or coworkers about my panic attacks." Richard shared with the Open Door support group that he had discussed his anxiety disorder with his employer as one of three employees applying for a promotion. Richard got the job. Obviously, his employer was more interested in his knowledge and skill than his panic attacks. Our anxiety problem may not carry as much weight as we think it does.

---

27 Weekes, *Hope and Help for Your Nerves,* page 33.

In our high-pressured society, where stress (anxiety) runs rampant, I hope employers become more accepting and understanding of those of us trying to cope with this problem. I hope employers come to realize that persons with anxiety are nonetheless dependable, conscientious and hard-working, an asset to the workplace.

I read the word "try" throughout the program. Shouldn't I just "do it"?
The word "try" has received a lot of bad press. If we say we're going to *try* to do something, people often assume that we probably won't do it. This may be true of the general public, but for those of us dealing with anxiety and panic attacks, *trying* is a good place to start. Few of us have the word "try" in our vocabulary.

"Do it!" is a problem because it is a command. It allows no retreat. Any excuse amounts to "copping out." But *try* is not a "cop out" word. *Try* is gentle. It allows for variation. *It allows for failure.* If we tell ourselves that we will at least try, and then be okay with the outcome, we put a lot less pressure on ourselves. Chances are, we will *just do it.*

In the following story, Marion feels pressured about taking a flight to Chicago. When she is told that she doesn't have to fly, that she can try another time, she has a last-minute change of mind.

Marion's Story
Marion, an Open Door support group member, took a fear of flying course. At the end of the three-day session, the class met for the graduation flight to Chicago. Marion

arrived at the airport and announced to the group that she was too anxious to make the trip, but wanted to cheer her classmates on.

Another Open Door member happened to be in the same class and said to Marion, "Of course you don't have to make the flight today. You can try another time when you're ready." As the class boarded the aircraft Marion joined them, much to everyone's surprise. Why had she changed her mind? Marion later explained that just knowing she had a choice took away the pressure. She realized that she didn't have to feel bad about not joining her class. With that in mind, she decided to try her best at flying.

(Programs for people with flying phobias include: www.flywithout fear.com, www.fearofflyingclinic.org, and myskyprogram.com)

Points to Remember: *Taking Risks*

1. We have the option of both staying and leaving a stressful situation. It's not what we do that is important, but what we tell ourselves about our decision.
2. Giving ourselves permission to leave without seeing it as failure relieves the feeling of being trapped, and makes it easier to return.
3. Taking risks is important because the more we avoid places where we feel anxious, the more difficult it is to face our fear.
4. When we see each risk we take as practice, there is no possibility of failure.

5. Being open about our anxiety or panic attacks takes away the fear of being found out.

6. "Try" is not a cop-out word. Rather, it is a gentle word. For those of us with anxiety, *trying* is a good place to begin.

Taking a Closer Look at Our Self-Talk

Recall a situation where you felt very anxious and wanted to leave.

1. Where were you and what was your decision?

2. What was your self-talk? Was it permissive of your feelings? Was it permissive of your decision?

3. If not, what might you have said to yourself that would have been more supportive?

(See suggested answers on page 102.)

How Do We Cope? *Riding as a Passenger in a Car*

What coping strategies would you use in the following situation?

Your office coworkers have decided to go out for lunch. You know that it will be difficult for you to join them. To make matters worse, you are invited to ride with them. You're not quite sure how to handle the situation, since you don't want them to know about your anxiety problem. *(See suggested answers on page 102.)*

More on Self-Talk: *Feeling the Fear and Taking the Risk*

What Am I Really Saying to Myself?

Here are three examples of how we might talk to ourselves when taking risks. Example 1 suggests what we might say to ourselves when planning to go into a feared situation. Example 2 tries logic and has high expectations. Example 3 sees the risk as practice and encourages us to allow the panic symptoms.

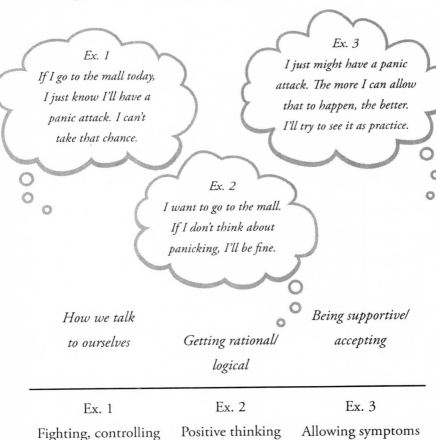

Ex. 1
If I go to the mall today, I just know I'll have a panic attack. I can't take that chance.

Ex. 2
I want to go to the mall. If I don't think about panicking, I'll be fine.

Ex. 3
I just might have a panic attack. The more I can allow that to happen, the better. I'll try to see it as practice.

How we talk to ourselves

Getting rational/ logical

Being supportive/ accepting

Ex. 1	Ex. 2	Ex. 3
Fighting, controlling	Positive thinking	Allowing symptoms

(Suggested answers for page 100.)

Taking a Closer Look at Our Self-Talk (question #3)

1. Even though going to the mall (restaurant, theater) was easy the last time, it doesn't necessarily mean I won't experience some anxiety today. I'll try to be okay with that.

2. If necessary, I can always leave. It will be good practice to give myself permission to do so.

3. I'm having a lot of anxiety lately. But since I've been taking more risks, that's to be expected.

4. The more I take risks, the better. I'm making progress even if I don't see immediate results.

How Do We Cope? Riding as a Passenger in a Car

Strategy A: I can choose not to go, telling them that I have some work I want to finish.

Strategy B: I can tell them that I prefer to drive and will meet them there.

Strategy C: I can ride with a coworker I trust, simply telling her that I'm not feeling well, and that I might need to leave during lunch.

GOALS, TIME LIMITS, SETBACKS

Rushing through the process of recovery is self-defeating
because it denies us the opportunity to learn and grow[28]

As anxiety or panic sufferers, we want to rid ourselves of our problem as quickly as possible, but are often frustrated in our attempts. Seeing the recovery process as linear, we set rigid goals, enforce time limits and hold high expectations. In spite of what appears to be a rational, step-by-step approach, we find that our progress is unpredictable and anything but quick. We are discouraged when we suddenly find ourselves in a setback (an unexpected recurrence of intense anxiety or panic attacks) and can't help but wonder what it is we're doing wrong.

Shouldn't I be setting goals for myself?
Setting goals can be important because they give us something to work toward. But it's the *working toward* that can create problems for us as perfectionists. If we have our mind set on working toward a particular goal, we may not be laid back in our approach, nor

---

28 Bemis and Barrada, *Embracing the Fear,* page 42.

have realistic expectations of either the process or the outcome. The prospect of failure can make us overly anxious.

Because of high expectations and all-or-nothing thinking, our goals tend to be unrealistic. We expect to see marked improvement with each passing day. Instead, we are faced with intense anxiety or unpredictable panic attacks, and struggle through the setbacks that are inevitable in the recovery process. Because goals usually involve deadlines, we find ourselves working against time, which may leave us frustrated and discouraged. For example, *I will be off of my medication by spring. I will be able to drive alone by the holidays. I want to travel this summer anxiety-free.*

If we put our recovery into a time frame, we add pressure that can actually slow down the process. By not accomplishing our goal in a given period of time, we may feel we have failed. In spite of our attempts to make it otherwise, we soon learn that the road to recovery is anything but smooth.

In the early days of Open Door, group members did set goals for themselves, sharing risks they wanted to take before the next meeting, such as crossing bridges, driving on the expressway, and staying home alone. I soon realized that they never discussed these goals at the following meetings. When I asked them why, they said they were embarrassed because they hadn't succeeded in reaching their goal during the allotted time period.

How long does recovery usually take?
Recovery takes time. How much is different for each person. It

helps to give it all the time it needs. Claire Weekes writes about the importance of taking recovery out of a time frame. She advises us not to be impatient, but to simply "let time pass."[29]

Letting time pass was important in my recovery. If necessary, I took my anxiety with me and did the best I could at the time, whether it was driving alone or going on vacation. I discovered that I could do pretty much anything I wanted to do as long as I was willing to be uncomfortable in the process. Not the discomfort that comes with white-knuckling or "putting up with," but the discomfort that comes with the reassurance that nothing is going to happen to me other than feeling anxious.

In the following story, Bev finds that there are no quick fixes when dealing with an anxiety disorder.

Bev's Story

The first night I went to my support group I felt hope. I sat quietly and listened. The aloneness I had been experiencing diminished. I heard that I wasn't the only one having those crazy feelings. Whew! What a relief! Naturally, I expected the quick cure. I would get these terrifying feelings in tow and get on with my life!

But that's not how recovery works.

Yet hope remains. Sometimes my day begins with fear, but the feeling is shorter-lived, nowhere near as intense, nor

---

29 Weekes. *Hope and Help for Your Nerves,* page 25.

does fear haunt me as often as it did in the past. I allow the fear to do whatever it needs to do, remembering always that it is only a feeling and that I am safe. Letting go takes practice, but it really has worked for me.

So many areas of my life have changed for the better. This program works! The difference is amazing when I keep my expectations low, stay with the panic feelings, and believe that they will pass. This is a process that moves slowly. No time limits. No quick fixes. But there is hope.

How can I avoid a setback?

It is only natural to want to avoid a setback, since a setback means having to deal with the intense anxiety or panic attacks all over again. However, we need to be open to that possibility. If not, our focus will be on protecting ourselves from regressing. For example, we know just how far we can go without experiencing symptoms and we are careful not to cross that line to avoid triggering a setback. In this case, avoidance is still protecting us from doing all that we want to do in our daily lives.

A setback could last anywhere from a few days to several months, or even longer. Feeling that our situation is hopeless, that we are trapped in a never-ending cycle of fear, we are discouraged and demoralized. But no matter how disturbing the setback might be, it is only temporary. Recognizing the source of the setback can be helpful. Perhaps we are going through a particularly stressful period—more pressure at work or a significant life change. In any case, we need to remind ourselves that setbacks are part of the recovery process and that we are still making progress. We might think of a setback as a time to continue practicing our coping skills.

Knowing that we can make it through a setback, gives us the confidence we need to handle future anxiety or panic attacks. In the following story, Rick talks about his setback and what he learned from it.

Rick's Story

Recently I experienced my first real setback. It pulled the rug out from under me. I felt I was right back where I started. It was very difficult to go through again, especially since I've been doing so well for such a long time. Since my setback started, I have had some major, but somewhat manageable, panic attacks, mood swings, and depression. But I've also made two changes.

Not until my setback did I realize how important B-talk was to me.[30] I think it's safe to say that A-talk has ruled. Now, with my new awareness, I'm using B-talk on a regular basis and hope to make it a more natural part of my life.

In addition, I'm seeing a therapist who has experience in working with anxiety disorders. In the past, I sometimes felt ashamed about seeing a therapist. Not this time. Instead of endlessly analyzing my situation myself, it helps to get

---

30 Bemis and Barrada, *Embracing the Fear,* page 31.

a professional opinion. I feel like I'm starting over, but I know that's not the case. I don't like the way I've been feeling, but I realize that it is a natural part of growth when dealing with anxiety.

This setback has been an experience, to say the least. Yet, if the only thing I learn from it is how I talk to myself, then it will all have been worth it. I now see how self-talk and acceptance are the foundation of this program.

Why are my panic attacks coming back? What should I do?
People have attended our support groups for several months and then dropped out. Six months later I'll receive a phone call: "The panic attacks are back! I thought I was through with all of this!" I hear the frustration in their voice. I remind them that recovery is not a smooth process, that anxiety or panic can rear its ugly head at any time. *Acceptance* is still the key word. I tell them that when we start feeling better, our expectations go up. We forget about allowing for setbacks or using a supportive and nurturing self-talk. We no longer think about slowing down and muddling through one day at a time when necessary.

I am no longer troubled by panic attacks. However, on several occasions I've had the feeling I would get just before an attack. On one occasion panic materialized, but the symptoms subsided within minutes. What is important is that these feelings have not caused me any concern. My first response each time has been, *Allow! Don't fight it! Just let it happen!* True, my anxiety level has gone up at times, but always for a reason. My reaction hasn't been, *Oh, no! Why is this happening?* Instead I have looked at what's going on in my life. I have asked myself such questions as, *Am I feeling overwhelmed by taking on too much? Do I need to slow down?* Then I have reminded myself, *Of course this is happening right now. Why wouldn't I feel this way? After all, this is how I react in situations like this. This is part of who I am.* This lack of concern says a lot to me because it is *fear* that feeds the anxiety or keeps the panic attacks waiting around the next corner.

If I don't keep practicing I'm afraid I'll lose ground

After all our efforts to get back on the highway, out to the mall or our favorite restaurant, we may suddenly find ourselves having a difficult time in any of these situations. We fear we are losing all the coping skills we've learned. To prevent this from happening, we keep pushing forward with the idea that *repeated practice will keep us from backtracking.* It's that old nonpermissive self-talk that doesn't let us go one day without holding our ground. It is easy to see how this vigilant attitude and perfectionistic self-talk can add to our anxiety.

Susan, a recovering agoraphobic, practiced her driving every day. After a car accident, she had to go for a prolonged period of time without her car. Her story illustrates how we can retain our coping skills even without daily practice.

Susan's Story

My car took six weeks to get fixed after an accident. Finally my husband went to pick it up. I had both longed for this moment and feared it. I just knew I had lost all my ability. I would be back to driving a few houses down my block, turning around and heading home.

I stood outside waiting for him, keys in hand, terrified.

As he pulled into the driveway, I began to tremble. This would be the test. I had not driven in six weeks. Could I still drive?

I got into my car and pulled out of the driveway. I was still fearful, but I got to the end of my block. Then I turned the corner and headed down to our main street. I could still drive! I won't say I was not anxious, but anyone who had been in an accident, who had not driven for a long time, would feel the same.

I've had my car back for over two weeks now and have lost nothing. My biggest fear did not come to pass. I can drive anywhere I was able to go before the accident. To me, the accident has become a life lesson and a very important one. I had no faith in how far I had come in my recovery. What I had learned was not transient. It was always with me.

Isn't a step-by-step approach used by some therapists?

Systematic desensitization is the name of a step-by-step process that takes us into the places we fear. For example, a person afraid of driving might begin desensitizing himself by sitting in his car without leaving the driveway. The next step could be driving to the end of the block and then adding distance with each practice session. Other places we fear, such as going to the mall, respond to this form of treatment as well. For example, we could drive as far as the mall parking lot, then turn around and go home. The next time, we could approach the entrance to the mall, and so on. Systematic desensitization is an important strategy in treating phobias, since facing fear is essential for recovery. However, even though it is built on increasing levels of exposure, we need to have realistic expectations.

When working with people who fear driving, I encourage them to simply drive in the direction of their destination, go as far as they want to and then turn around. This takes away the pressure of having to achieve a fixed goal, and removes the fear of failure. The next time we go out, expectations are high: *Well, the last time I went ten blocks, so today I should be able to go at least eleven.* I caution them that each practice session is different and that it is important to lower their expectations and allow for less than ten blocks. Every block is practice.

Some time ago, I gave a presentation on anxiety to a group of college students and brought up the topic of systematic desensitization. A woman in the class questioned the effectiveness of this kind of therapy. She was still having panic attacks behind the wheel even after driving for five years. She wanted to know why her driving wasn't getting easier. I asked her what she was saying to herself each time she got into her car. She answered, "What if I panic?" This kind of self-talk tells me that her focus was on staying in control rather than allowing for the possibility of an attack. It was important for her to face her fear by taking the risk of driving. However, a permissive self-talk would have helped her drive with less anxiety.

How can I tell if I'm improving?

If our treatment were surgical, we could see ourselves progressively getting better post-operatively with each passing day. But with an anxiety disorder, it is difficult to measure day-to-day progress. We have good days and bad days, reach plateaus, and then suddenly hit a setback. Recovery is anything but smooth. But there are ways that tell us whether we're improving despite the ups and downs of recovery, ways that measure our progress over time.

For one, we may find ourselves going places and doing things we hadn't been able to do for a long time. I remember going to a restaurant with my husband. After dinner I looked around and realized that we were sitting at a table in the middle of the room surrounded by other diners. Being too far from the door always made me anxious, so this was something I hadn't done in quite a while. Yet panicking hadn't occurred to me the entire time. Suddenly I wondered, *When and how did this happen?*

Another way we notice progress is through family and friends. We forget about our struggles and fail to appreciate our progress. It's their feedback that tells us how well we're doing. It has been a long time since I dealt with anxiety and panic attacks with agoraphobia, but every now and then I'm reminded of the progress I've made.

Judy's Story

My stepdaughter was visiting from Colorado. During her visit, we attended a show at the Ordway Music Theatre in St. Paul. Moving in and out of crowded corridors, she turned to me and said, "You're really handling crowds well." I wasn't sure what she meant. Then it dawned on me: As long as she had known me, I had had a difficult time being in crowds. I avoided them by arriving at the theatre early, sitting near the door, waiting for them to disperse before leaving. Or else I avoided crowded places entirely. Her comment gave me reason to reflect on how far I had come and how much I now took for granted. Looking back, it was a permissive self-talk, based on acceptance, that allowed me to move at my own pace without time limits.

As I progress in my recovery, I resent all that I missed out on
  because of my anxiety

It is not uncommon to feel resentment about what our anxiety has cost us. I felt that sense of loss in my own recovery. Although I kept fairly active, which required a lot of white-knuckling, I missed out on many things because of fear: social activities, classes, and outings with my family.

I felt a special sense of loss when I thought of lost opportunities. My children were grown and it was too late for that walk in the park. My mother had died and we could no longer travel together. She once asked me to go on a bus tour with her. The thought of riding on a bus for three hours kept me from ever sharing that experience with her. With such lost opportunities in mind, and in the midst of sadness, we can gently remind ourselves of the many other experiences we *did* share and feel grateful for them. We can also appreciate the many things that we are able to do now.

Recently, I took my grandson to a park. While we played Frisbee amidst crowds of people I asked myself, *Why are we here at the park when we could be doing this in the privacy of our own backyard?* Suddenly, it occurred to me that I was doing something with my grandson that I hadn't been able to do with my own children. When my two daughters were preschoolers we lived only a few blocks from a park. But because of my panic attacks, there were times when I couldn't take them there. Being at the park with my grandson now took on a whole new meaning.

As our anxiety or panic attacks subside over time, we can experience such a wonderful sense of freedom that we no longer think much about regrets. We simply immerse ourselves in the process of living.

Points to Remember: *Goals, Time Limits, Setbacks*

1. Goals and time limits tend to add pressure and can slow down the recovery process.
2. Because of our high expectations and all-or-nothing thinking we expect to see marked improvement with each passing day.
3. Systematic desensitization is an important strategy in treating phobias, since facing our fear is essential to recovery.

THE POWER OF ACCEPTANCE

4. We can have good days and bad days, reach plateaus, and then suddenly struggle through a setback. This inconsistency makes it difficult to measure our progress.

5. Even though we might fear a setback, the best thing we can do is to be open to the possibility.

6. It will help if we try to take one day at a time, muddling through when necessary. Seeing a setback as temporary, we can remind ourselves: This too shall pass.

7. When our expectations rise, we tend to forget about allowing for setbacks or using a supportive and nurturing self-talk. We forget about slowing down and muddling through as needed.

Taking a Closer Look at Our Self-Talk

Setbacks can be discouraging, but they are a necessary part of
the recovery process.

1. What might be happening in my life to cause a setback?

2. When I am discouraged about my progress, what happens to my self-talk?

3. What self-talk might I use to help me through a setback?

(See suggested answers on page 118.)

How Do We Cope? *Dealing with a Time Limit*

What strategies would you use in the following situation?

Your family is planning a vacation within the next few months. You are going through a setback and you really don't want to travel too far away from home. In addition, your family is counting on you to join them. You know that you have three months before the big event. *(See suggested answers on page 118.)*

More on Self-Talk: *Goals, Time Limits, Setbacks*
What Am I Really Saying to Myself?
Here are three examples of how we might talk to ourselves during a setback. In example 1 we see our alarm at having regressed. Example 2 tries to be rational and places recovery in a time frame. Example 3 accepts the setback as a normal part of the recovery process and reassures us that we are still making progress.

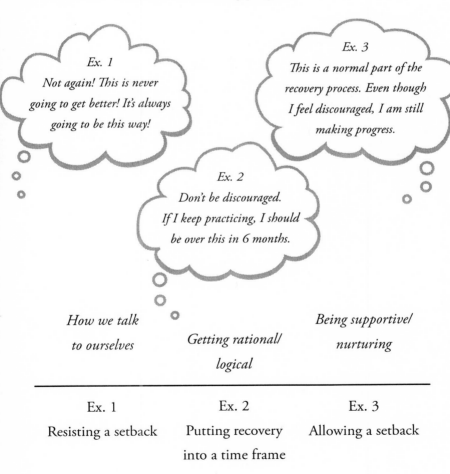

Ex. 1
Not again! This is never going to get better! It's always going to be this way!

Ex. 3
This is a normal part of the recovery process. Even though I feel discouraged, I am still making progress.

Ex. 2
Don't be discouraged. If I keep practicing, I should be over this in 6 months.

How we talk to ourselves	*Getting rational/ logical*	*Being supportive/ nurturing*
Ex. 1	Ex. 2	Ex. 3
Resisting a setback	Putting recovery into a time frame	Allowing a setback

(Suggested answers for pages 115, 116.)

Taking a Closer Look at Our Self-Talk (question #3)

1. I can deal with this one day at a time. Today I'll try to be patient with my progress.

2. The more I take my time in recovery, the better. Trying to rush through the process is not helpful. I can try to see this as a time to continue practicing helpful coping strategies. I am still making progress.

3. It has been quite a while since I've felt this anxious, but it makes a lot of sense considering the recent stresses in my life (the pressures at work, family conflict, financial difficulties, etc.).

4. It will help if I accept where I'm at in my recovery.

How Do We Cope? Dealing with a Time Limit

Strategy A: Expecting to make the trip anxiety-free after only a few months is not realistic. So I'll try to allow as much time as needed for my recovery and plan to travel with some discomfort if necessary. The more willing I am to do this, the better my chances of making the trip.

Strategy B: I can plan to give myself a "last-minute out" (and be up front with my family about my plans). That will help to alleviate some of the anticipatory anxiety. In the meantime, I'll continue to practice my coping skills.

CHAPTER THREE

ACCEPTANCE IN EVERYDAY LIFE

*If I could just take away the need to rush
into each new day full speed ahead
in order to accomplish all the shoulds
on my ever-growing list. I want to slow down
the rushing of my mind and keep it from
running away from fear.*

*Journal entry
February, 1984*

ACCEPTANCE IN EVERYDAY LIFE

I continually avoided places where I experienced panic attacks
until I finally realized that my biggest fear was fear

In chapter 2, "The Power of Acceptance," we discussed seven different strategies for dealing with anxiety and panic attacks: acceptance, permissive self-talk, allowing our symptoms, slowing down, lowering expectations, removing time limits, and allowing for setbacks. Acceptance forms the basis of all the strategies. In this chapter, we put them to work for us in a number of situations where we often experience anxiety or panic attacks. The overlap among these strategies will be clear. There are just so many ways you can say "accept" and "allow."

I'm afraid to travel too far from home
Many of us have a difficult time with travel. We see it as a risk. Not only are we anxious leaving our safe place, but being between our point of departure and our destination can feel like a "no-safety zone." We anticipate being anxious or panicky here because we think there is nowhere to turn for help. Our destination can also be a source of anxiety. We don't always know what to expect once we arrive.

We are often "territorial." We believe that as long as we are within our territory we can keep the anxiety or panic attacks at bay. Our no-safety zone could be just outside the city limits, outside our neighborhood or outside our house. Fear of anxiety or panic has a strong hold on us. Yet as long as we are afraid, we give it power, and it will be waiting for us around the next corner.

When traveling, a permissive inner dialogue will make it easier to take the risk: *It's okay to be anxious. It's good practice for me to take risks. There is help if I need it. However, I will be okay. I'll try to deal with each new experience as it happens.* A travel partner might also help, someone who is patient, understanding, and willing to turn around and return home at anytime.

The following story illustrates the importance of taking risks.

Mary's Story

Travel was the last hurdle in my recovery. I was convinced that panic waited for me on the other side of my self-imposed boundaries, the city limits. I felt trapped. The fear of having a panic attack kept me close to home for a long time. When I was willing to take the risk of traveling, I started out with weekend getaways with my husband, such as a nearby bed and breakfast. I didn't wait for my anxiety and panic attacks to go away before venturing out, but accepted the fact that, for now, I would have to take them with me. By this time I had developed a self-talk that was permissive of my symptoms, one that reassured me that nothing would happen to me other than the panic itself. My territorial perimeters slowly expanded and I found it well worth the risks I was taking.

I'm afraid to drive on the freeway

First of all, we don't need to drive on highways or freeways. They might be the quickest and simplest way to get where we are going, but they aren't the only way. The back roads or side streets will get us there too. We just need to give ourselves permission—without guilt or shame—to take an alternative route. With time and practice, we will be able to drive on highways and freeways without a problem.

Just as with travel, a support person can help us as we begin practicing freeway driving. We need someone who understands our fear. I remember working with a woman who had a difficult time driving outside of the city limits, especially on a particular two-lane road with oncoming traffic at high speed. She felt trapped because she thought she couldn't stop the car when she wanted to. This of course made her feel panicky. While doing some practice driving, I encouraged her to pull over to the side of the road every few miles until it felt natural for her to do so. Once she realized she had that option, she no longer felt trapped and could drive with less anxiety.

In the following, Sandy shares her experience with driving on inner-city streets as well as the highway.

Sandy's Story

I remember when I thought nothing of driving from St. Paul

to New York City. I loved driving alone with my thoughts and the sound of the radio. I felt a sense of freedom and sought out new places and adventures. That is, up until my first panic attack. Soon, my car just sat in the driveway. I was too afraid to drive. My colleagues drove me to and from work.

After several months I got behind the wheel again. At first I just drove around the block, adding a few blocks at a time. Some days I was terrified. My fear of driving alone didn't make any sense to me. I had traveled on the highway at any time of night or day. Now, just driving past entrance ramps made me shudder. I couldn't understand what had happened.

When I was finally able to drive myself to work, I knew the location of every public telephone en route so I could stop and call for help. I took the back roads religiously, even if it meant going out of my way. I even learned how to avoid left-hand turns at traffic lights.

Eventually, I was ready to take the risk of highway driving again. I began one exit at a time. Once on the ramp, I was trapped until the next exit, which seemed miles away. Feeling the panic rise, I would floor the accelerator to get off the highway as quickly as I could. I had not yet learned to *escape slowly*, to allow the anxiety symptoms. I had no inner dialogue other than *Oh, my god* and *What if.*

We may be embarrassed about avoiding the highway or freeway, but nowhere is it carved in stone that we must travel from one place to another by any particular route. When we tell ourselves that we *should* be able to drive on the freeway, we create a problem. It might help to remind ourselves that there are nonphobic drivers who choose to avoid the highway or freeway, especially during rush hour. They have no problem making that decision because it makes perfect sense to them. In time, we learn to make our own rules.

Is it true that what works on the ground works in the air?
One of our problems with air travel is coping with the time between point A and point B. Even a forty-five minute flight can seem like an eternity. The cabin door closes and we feel trapped. The entire flight is spent pretending we're somewhere else (denial), counting patterns on the seat in front of us (distraction), reciting statistics on the safety of flying (rational thinking), or dulling our senses with alcohol or tranquilizers (avoidance). We brace ourselves against every tilt and turn, and react with alarm to an unfamiliar sound or the least bit of turbulence. Our desperate attempts to stay in control can make the trip even more uncomfortable.

When we make our travel arrangements, it might help to choose an aisle seat so that we're able to move around the plane more easily, one directly behind first class seating where the engine noise is lower and the flight is smoother. Rather than build up resistance by gripping the armrests and tensing every muscle, we can try to allow ourselves to go with the motion of the plane.

My breakthrough occurred when I took an actual flight with a therapist. It wasn't easy to do the flight, but I learned an important lesson: what works on the ground, such as in malls and on highways, can work as well at 35,000 feet.

Judy's Story

I had been a fearful flyer for twenty-five years. Finally, I contacted a local therapist and arranged for a forty-five-minute flight to Milwaukee. We met the day before the flight and his advice had a familiar ring to it. "Allow yourself to be anxious." Even though I knew from experience that this strategy worked on the ground, I had a difficult time trusting that it would be effective in the air.

The next morning, as the aircraft was taking off, my heart was pounding and my hands were wet. Suddenly, I reached across the aisle and grabbed hold of his arm. In a very casual voice he asked, "Have you looked out the window yet, Judy?" This had never occurred to me, but as he spoke, my head turned and I could see the ground getting farther away. I had hoped he would offer me words of comfort. Instead, he was challenging me to stay in touch with my surroundings.

Later in the flight, the therapist asked, "Are you up here at 35,000 feet or are you home in your favorite chair?" Poof! There went my favorite chair. Suddenly I had to face the fact that I was in a jet plane 35,000 feet off the ground. But instead of resisting, I sat back and allowed my anxiety to be there. It was a feeling of total surrender. During all those years of flying I had spent the entire flight trying hard to block out my anxiety. Now I realized that my biggest fear was the fear itself. I didn't want to be trapped with those panicky feelings for any length of time. Allowing myself to be afraid was a turning point. Since that flight, I've been able to fly with little or no anxiety.

What can I do about family gatherings?
We may anticipate upcoming family gatherings with a great deal of anxiety. We don't know what to expect. Already sensitized, we must face the possibility of crowded conditions, an accelerated noise level and our own high expectations of appearing relaxed (or as our non-permissive self-talk might say, appearing "normal"). Not wanting anyone to suspect that we have an anxiety problem, we feel we must hide any of our symptoms for fear of being judged or ridiculed. If the family is aware of our situation, there's usually one relative who will ask, "Do you still have that problem?" or "When are you going to get over this?" Or add such unhelpful advice as, "Just don't think about it. You'll be fine! Just do it!" This only reinforces the message we have already been giving ourselves: *Something's wrong with me! I shouldn't have this problem! I have to stop being so anxious!*

In order to make family gatherings easier, we need to feel okay about ourselves in spite of the lack of understanding surrounding us. We do not have to explain our situation to anyone, nor do we have to make excuses or feel embarrassed. It is important that we establish boundaries and stand up to those who are quick to judge us or give unhelpful advice. If necessary, they must be told that their response is inappropriate. We could say, "I'm sorry you feel that way, but I'm really pleased with my progress," or "I'm sure this is difficult for you to understand but it's really beginning to make a lot of sense to me." It will be easier to make these statements when we have reached a point where we can accept our anxiety problem and still feel good about ourselves.

It will also help if we can give ourselves permission to leave and find a place where we can be alone if we so choose, a place where we don't have to be on guard or keep up small talk. Giving ourselves the freedom to come and go as we please can help alleviate some anxiety.

Of course, we do have the option of not attending these functions even though we feel pressured to do so. Unfortunately, avoiding family gatherings can be a no-win situation, since we may feel guilty for not attending. Here again, our self-talk can come to the rescue by reassuring us that, given our circumstances, it is okay to make that decision.

What if I have to attend a family funeral?

Many anxiety sufferers, especially those of us with agoraphobia, worry about being unable to attend a family funeral. In addition to our own personal need to attend, we feel a great deal of outside pressure. We find it difficult to permit ourselves to do otherwise.

However, we need to give ourselves the option of not attending. *What if I were ill and simply could not go?* we might ask ourselves. If so, we would most likely stay home. But since we are dealing with anxiety, a compassionate and nurturing self-talk is needed to give ourselves permission to stay home the day of the funeral.

On the other hand, if we do decide to go, we will need to draw on a number of coping strategies to help us through this difficult situation. It will help to have low expectations and a self-talk that not only allows the anxiety that will most likely be present, but a self-talk that gives us permission to leave the service at any time. It will also help to have support people to rely on.

Whether we attend the funeral or not, it will be difficult. We will need to be gentle with ourselves and use a self-talk that supports our decision. A lot will depend on where we are in our recovery and our willingness to put ourselves through the emotional and physical discomfort.

Colette's Story

One of the most difficult challenges I have had to face since becoming agoraphobic is going to my father's funeral. My father had advanced cancer so his death did not come as a complete surprise. I had asked my therapist how to cope with a funeral. For example, should I take twice my normal dose of anti-anxiety medication before leaving my house? She recommended that I take the usual amount but carry an extra dose as a precaution if I felt my anxiety increasing.

She suggested leaving the room for another room or hallway in the funeral parlor, if necessary. She also suggested asking for a hug, telling someone that I was anxious, and using diaphragmatic breathing.

So what actually happened? I had trouble sleeping the night before and was anxious before leaving the house. This was to be expected. I took my normal dose of medication. My husband was supportive on the drive to the funeral home for the visitation; he told me, "You think that you have to stay for all of this, but you really don't." His words and his presence were comforting. Several times, my anxiety rose and fell during the visitation. I received hugs, and conversation distracted me from my fears. Twice when my husband was away from my side, I asked friends to come and stand or sit with me. This was very helpful.

The worst part was the funeral itself. In the middle of the eulogy, every cell of my body told me to leave. I experienced a panic attack of ten based on a scale of one to ten. Most unpleasant was the sensation of the room spinning. I prayed, "Please God, help me." My husband held my left hand, and my niece held my right. I had a glass of water ready and took the extra medication during the eulogy. My anxiety was at its peak. Maybe I should have taken it sooner because it was then of no help.

I was pleased that I could attend the funeral out of love for my father and to support my mother. I stayed for all of it but wish it had been easier. It was difficult but, as you can see, not impossible.

How can I possibly leave work?

It is difficult enough dealing with anxiety and panic attacks on the home front, but it is even more difficult to deal with them in the workplace. It can be one of our biggest challenges. Since we don't want our boss or coworkers to know about our problem, we feel we can't possibly leave our desk when we are anxious or panicking. Yet the more we tell ourselves, *I have to stay here, I can't leave,* the more of a problem it becomes. It is important to recognize that just because we tell ourselves we *can* leave doesn't mean that we are going to do it. The fact is, by giving ourselves that option, we most likely won't have to leave. Giving ourselves an option alleviates the feeling of entrapment.

If we were to come down with the flu or have a severe headache, we wouldn't hesitate to leave work. We wouldn't consider it unusual or inappropriate because we see a physical illness—but not anxiety—as valid. We are afraid that once we allow ourselves to go home, a pattern will develop and repeat itself until we face the prospect of losing our job. Although this is possible, it isn't necessarily true. Remember the story about Richard who told his boss about his anxiety disorder and was still offered a promotion? Being open about our anxiety with our supervisor, or a coworker, might make it easier to stay on the job, since we no longer have to hide our problem. Having a "safe person" at work can also be helpful. For a long time I had a safe person where I worked. It felt secure knowing that I could go to his office, if necessary, and tell him that I needed help.

I have a difficult time giving a presentation

Public speaking is difficult for most people. Being the center of attention can be stressful, even without an anxiety problem. We want to perform well and appear confident. We are afraid that we will look anxious, have a memory lapse, and make a fool of ourselves. We feel trapped. We can't just stop in our tracks and leave. Just thinking about it causes intense anxiety. All we can think about is how to get out of speaking altogether.

Though we may insist on giving the perfect presentation, we need to give ourselves permission to make mistakes, to be anxious, even to the point of looking uncomfortable. We need to give ourselves options about how we present our material. This not only helps us manage the anxiety, but can help prevent feeling trapped. The effectiveness of these strategies is illustrated in the following story.

Greg's Story

I had to give a presentation at work, which caused me a great deal of anticipatory anxiety. Finally, I asked myself what I was afraid of, what was the worst thing that could happen? The answer was simple: I was afraid that I would look anxious, that I wouldn't be able to utter a sound, or at best, would stumble over every word. I was afraid I would look incompetent.

But once I knew what my fear was, I could see what I needed to do about it. I made sure I was well prepared so that I was familiar with the material. During the presentation, I used slides to direct some of the attention away from myself. I divided my material up into ten-minute segments so that I could have closure at any time. Most important, I kept my expectations low by giving myself permission to appear anxious, since that was my main concern. By doing so I felt less pressure and got through the presentation with less anxiety.

As usual, I discovered that the anticipation was worse than the actual event.

What if I have to go to the hospital for medical reasons?
Going to the hospital for medical procedures, such as surgery, can be challenging for us. Hospitals present us with unfamiliar environments and people: waiting rooms, elevators, roommates and hospital staff we don't know. Separated from family, friends, and familiar surroundings, we feel as though we are in a vacuum. Hooked up to medical equipment, we feel trapped. Our anxiety increases as we anticipate further tests and treatments.

So how do we deal with these challenges? First, we need to trust those in charge, and reassure ourselves that we will be well cared for. Second, we must make our needs known so that we feel more in control of the situation. Doctors and nurses should be aware that we are dealing with (or have dealt with) an anxiety disorder and that we would like procedures explained to us in some detail (or not explained at all, as the case may be). Third, it might make our anxiety easier to manage if we try to break each day into blocks of time. If we are able to do this, we will only have to think about the morning's procedures and deal with the afternoon when it comes. Finally, if we are left alone waiting for x-rays or other medical procedures, we need a way to get in touch with the nurse or technician in charge so that we don't feel isolated. We can also see to it that we will not be left alone *before* we are taken to a procedure, rather than trying to get help once we've been dropped off.

In any case, it will help to be permissive of our anxiety and remember that this, too, shall pass. Despite the challenges of surgery or other medical procedures, we need to surrender to what seems to be an overwhelming situation. In the following story, Dan finds effective ways to get through his MRI despite his anxiety.

Dan's Story

Recently I had an MRI scan. I made it a point to tell the technician that I was claustrophobic and had a history of panic disorder. Though the MRI was open-sided, I wanted out within sixty seconds. The technician suggested putting a wet wash cloth over my eyes and pretending I was somewhere else. I knew that wouldn't work. Then he offered to reschedule so I could be medicated before the procedure.

But I had another idea. I asked him if he could adjust the height of the table so I would have extra space inside the machine. I also asked if he would stay in the room so that I could come out at any time. He agreed to do both. I was still anxious, but decided to give it a try.

Thirty-five minutes later the scan was complete. The technician remarked that people usually won't go back in once they've decided they don't like it. "What did you say to yourself?" he asked. I told him that I reassured myself that I didn't have to be embarrassed about my anxiety or about asking for what I needed. I also explained that I gave myself permission to be anxious, even if it meant failing at my second attempt. With this permission I felt some control over the situation and it made a big difference.

I'm afraid to stay by myself

Staying home alone is a problem for many of us when we are feeling anxious or anticipating panic attacks. One of our biggest fears is being isolated and unable to get help. Anxiety and panic attacks are frightening enough when we are with family or friends, but alone, we obsess about the possibility that no one will be there to help us.

Alone with our thoughts we focus on such self-talk as, *What if I panic and can't get to the phone? What if I pass out and there's no one to help me?* Now more than ever we need a nurturing and reassuring inner dialogue, for example, *If I panic, I panic. Nothing terrible is going to happen to me. There will be time to get to the phone if necessary. Someone will help me.*

In the early stages of an anxiety disorder it is especially frightening to be alone since we are still convinced that our problem is physical and that we are in some kind of danger. I remember when I first started having panic attacks. I actually drove to the hospital one night and sat outside the emergency room so that I would be close to medical help. Those early days and nights were terrifying. I didn't want to be alone, but I was afraid to tell my family that I was having unexplainable symptoms that seemed to be coming from out of nowhere. So I muddled through the best I could on my own. I weathered a number of panic attacks and saw the inside of more than one emergency room before I was finally convinced that I wasn't dying. In time, I built up enough confidence to feel safe on my own again.

The problem is compounded when we have young children. We not only question our ability to care for ourselves under these circumstances, but we are afraid we won't be able to function as a parent. In a sensitized state it is so easy to lose confidence in our ability to cope.

One suggestion is to have the phone number of a family member or friend. Just knowing we can reach someone can alleviate the feeling of isolation. Other suggestions include inviting friends over, planning activities, or becoming involved in a project. This may be challenging, because it is difficult to focus on anything when we're anxious or depressed. Although diversions won't necessarily solve our problem, they remind us that we don't have to feel stuck at home alone with nothing to think about but our anxiety.

Karen's Story

I was a young mother suffering with panic attacks. My husband was out of town for the weekend. By late Saturday afternoon anxiety had overwhelmed me. I paced the floor, worrying that something would happen to me and no one would be there to take care of my children. In desperation, I said out loud, "Someone please help me!" My two-year-old, who I didn't know was close by, ran to my side and took my hand. "I'll help you, mommy," she said. Not wanting to frighten her, I gathered her up in my arms and reassured her that mommy would be fine. In doing so, I reassured myself as well and decided that it would be a good idea to call a friend. Not only was she sympathetic, but she offered to come over and stay with me until my husband arrived home. I declined, but felt more secure knowing that someone was there for me if needed.

I feel more anxious when the weather gets hot

It is not uncommon for people with anxiety to struggle with hot weather. The discomfort of high humidity is similar to anxiety symptoms: a feeling of smothering, dizziness, sweating, or light-headedness. Although such feelings are not reserved for those of us with an anxiety problem, we tend to magnify the feelings. Each symptom is interpreted as ominous. It is important that we remind ourselves not to attach danger to the symptoms and just allow ourselves to experience the physical discomfort.

What-if questions abound: *What if I'm overcome with the heat? What if the car breaks down and I'm stranded?* I've asked myself these same questions, and given myself the following answers: *Of course I feel this way. Why wouldn't I? This is how I react to the heat. It is perfectly normal for me to feel like this. Everyone experiences discomfort in intense heat.*

For those of us who have a problem with soaring temperatures, we can take precautions by dressing appropriately, drinking extra liquids, and taking advantage of fans or air conditioning.

Points to Remember: *Acceptance in Everyday Life*

1. Allowing ourselves to be anxious will help us when traveling, since our biggest challenge is fear of fear. We might remind ourselves that we are not in any danger, that we carry our safety within.

2. We seem to think that we should be able to drive on the highway. However, back roads or side streets can serve our purpose. We just need to give ourselves permission to make that decision without feeling embarrassed.

3. In order to make family gatherings easier, it will help if we can be more accepting of our anxiety problem and feel good about ourselves in spite of it.

4. It is important to establish boundaries with friends and relatives who are quick to judge us or give us unhelpful advice.

5. Giving ourselves permission to leave work when we are anxious or panicky can actually make it easier to stay.

6. It might help to confide in a coworker about our anxiety or panic

attacks so that we won't feel a constant need to hide our problem.

7. When having medical procedures, it will help to let the staff know that we have anxiety or panic attacks. It is okay to ask for what we need, such as having procedures explained to us.

8. During a hospital stay, it might help to break the day up into blocks so that we only have to think about one procedure at a time.

9. When staying alone, we might consider keeping the phone number of a friend or family member handy so we won't feel so isolated.

Taking a Closer Look at Our Self-Talk

Recall a time when you were alone or anticipated being alone.

1. What was your greatest fear?

2. What was your was self-talk?

3. What could you have said to yourself to make it easier to cope with your anxiety on your own?

(See suggested answers on page 141.)

How Do We Cope? *Planning a Trip*

What strategies would you use?

You are planning a short trip that will involve two hours of driving. At this stage of your recovery, it's like driving halfway around the globe. Although you have a traveling companion, you're not sure whether you can do it. You're afraid you might panic on the way. Besides, even if you do make it to your destination, you're afraid you won't be able to get home again. *(See suggested answers on page 141.)*

More on Self-Talk: *Acceptance in Everyday Life*

What Am I Really Saying to Myself?

Here are three examples of how we might talk to ourselves when staying alone. Example 1 is typical of how we might respond when feeling isolated, with no help at hand. Example 2 seems logical since it attempts to stop the frightening thoughts. Example 3 accepts our feelings of isolation and need for support. It allows for any anxiety that might occur and reassures us that help is closer than we sometimes think.

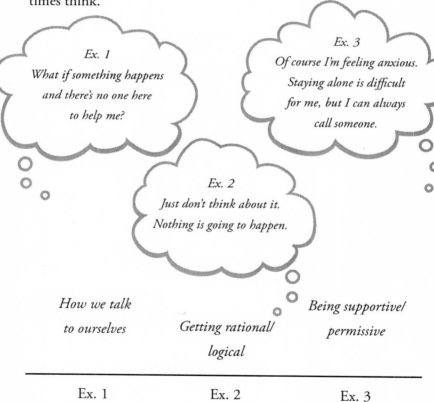

Ex. 1
What if something happens and there's no one here to help me?

Ex. 3
Of course I'm feeling anxious. Staying alone is difficult for me, but I can always call someone.

Ex. 2
Just don't think about it. Nothing is going to happen.

How we talk to ourselves — *Getting rational/ logical* — *Being supportive/ permissive*

Ex. 1	Ex. 2	Ex. 3
Anticipating anxiety	Thought stopping	Accepting, allowing

(Suggested answers for page 139.)

Taking a Closer Look at Our Self-Talk (question #3)

1. If I panic, I panic. Nothing will happen to me. I will be okay!

2. There will be time to get to the phone if necessary. Someone will help me.

3. It is good practice for me to be on my own. I will be able to handle any anxiety I might experience.

4. I do not have to do this on my own. I have the option of staying with a friend or asking someone to come over.

How Do We Cope? Planning a Trip

Strategy A: I know that blocking out my anxiety, pretending it isn't there, won't work for me. The best thing I can do is to acknowledge the fact that I'm anxious and take my anxiety with me. Allowing the anxiety, at any point in the trip, will be more helpful than trying to block it out.

Strategy B: I might remind myself that even though this isn't easy for me, it is still my choice to make this trip. I'll keep my expectations low and muddle through the best I can. I can change my mind at the last minute. If that happens, I'll try to be okay with my decision.

CHAPTER FOUR
GROWING IN AWARENESS

She walks cautiously for she is afraid. Don't criticize her.
She has become an expert at that herself.
Ask her how she feels. Perhaps she'll tell you.
Ask her what she thinks. She just might have an opinion.
Give her space...and she will grow.

Journal Entry
February, 1975

GROWING IN AWARENESS

Our anxiety isn't just coming from out of the blue.
There's a reason why we're having these feelings[31]

My therapist once asked me, "What do you think about before you have a panic attack?" I couldn't understand why he would ask that question. I was sure nothing in particular would cross my mind. The attacks, I explained, came from out of nowhere. He then suggested that I try to be aware of my thoughts just before the next attack.

At first I didn't have much success realizing those thoughts, but as time went on it got easier. I discovered that it wasn't so much a thought as a feeling—a sense of being cut off, of being isolated. At times it was a feeling of helplessness, of not being in charge of my environment.

We can gain such an awareness of what might be triggering our anxiety or panic by asking ourselves the following questions:

- Do I feel safe expressing my thoughts and opinions, or is it better if I keep silent and not risk being criticized, or worse yet, rejected?

---

31 Bemis and Barrada, *Cards for Releasing Fear & Anxiety.*

145

- Do I allow myself to express emotions such as anger or disappointment, or is it more important to always be nice?
- Do I need constant approval from others in order to feel good about myself?
- Am I able to make decisions, assert myself and establish boundaries when necessary?
- Am I able to meet conflict head on and try to resolve it, or is it easier for me to walk away and avoid it entirely to keep the peace?
- In other words, do I feel in charge of my life, or do I feel powerless, as if nothing I do can make a difference?

In this chapter, we will take a look at these questions. By answering them, we will discover that our anxiety or panic attacks do not come from out of the blue. They are there for a reason. They are trying to tell us something.

Getting in Touch With our Feelings

Long before our first panic attack, many of us learned to detach ourselves from such emotions as sadness, loneliness, anger, and disappointment. We convinced ourselves that they weren't so important. After all, everyone experiences these feelings at one time or another. Minimizing them was a way of protecting ourselves from having to face them. I remember once making the comment, "All I have to do is turn my feelings off like a light switch." I was referring to the end of a long, meaningful relationship. Although I tried hard to move into a state of total denial, the pain ran deep. Finally it erupted, along with all my other unresolved feelings, in the form of my first panic attack.

The ability to become aware of and express our feelings is an essential part of recovering from an anxiety disorder.[32] However, expressing how we feel doesn't always feel safe. For many of us, expressing our feelings was neither expected nor appreciated when we were growing up. Being able to talk openly about feelings is something we learn.

Anger is a commonly repressed emotion, probably because it wasn't acceptable to express anger when we were children. It was associated with disrespect and loss of control. Expressing anger, or even feeling angry, can still be disturbing to us. Not only do we feel out of control, it doesn't fit our self-image, that "nice" person we think we're supposed to be. We've learned that it's best to keep such feelings in check.

Grief is a powerful, emotional response to loss. It can leave us feeling distraught, helpless, out of control. We switch from facing the stark reality of our loss to the numbness of denial, struggling to keep our balance. To avoid the pain we may try to repress it. But we must go through the process of grieving in order to heal and eventually move on. Harder yet, there seems to be an unwritten time limit for expressing our grief. Friends are sympathetic up to a point and then we are expected to get on with our lives. But the sadness may run deep and last long beyond anyone's expectations.

---

32 Bourne, *Anxiety & Phobia Workbook,* page 256.

Moreover, some of us hold beliefs that can complicate the grieving process: *grieving shows weakness* or *grieving shows a lack of spiritual faith.* It is important that we allow ourselves to experience our emotions, but such beliefs encourage us to repress them. A grief support group can ease the process. Someone from the group is always available to listen, someone who understands and shares the grief experience, regardless of how long it lasts.

Taking Charge of our Lives

It is not uncommon for us to be in a relationship that is out of balance. People with anxiety disorders may be less likely to take charge of their lives when it comes to, say, handling money, or making important decisions. Not wanting to make a mistake and face criticism, we choose not to make decisions at all. Hesitant to speak up or express opinions, we find it easier to remain passive and just walk away from any chance of conflict. Perhaps because we don't take the initiative, the other person feels the need to take charge.

We tend to see our spouses or partners as emotionally stronger, and more capable of handling matters in general. As we become more dependent on them, we can reach a point where we no longer trust our own judgment. When this happens, our self-esteem suffers and we lose confidence in our ability to function on an adult level. We may feel stuck because we see no way out of our dilemma. Increased anxiety can leave us open to panic.

In the following story, Diane, who struggled with agoraphobia for almost twelve years, discovers that she has less anxiety when she feels more in charge of her life.

Diane's Story

I remember taking the recycling bin out to the curb. It was 5:30 a.m. There, in the quiet of the early morning, it suddenly occurred to me that I was capable of performing this mundane chore on my own. *I can do this!* I thought, with a feeling of accomplishment. Since my husband and I had separated I was discovering that I could do a lot of things. I could make decisions on my own, manage money, keep up the house, and hold down a full-time job. I was actually taking charge of my life. During our ten years of marriage, how could I have allowed things get so out of hand? With my lack of assertiveness and fear of confrontation I realized that I was part of the problem.

"How would you rate your marriage on a scale of one to ten?" a therapist asked me. "About an eight," I answered without hesitation. At the end of the session, after discussing my difficulty in keeping a balanced relationship, he asked me again, "Now how would you rate your marriage?" I looked at him helplessly and said, "About a five?"

Whether I try to make another go of this marriage or start a new relationship altogether, I will have to learn to be more assertive, to be more willing to express my feelings, and to set boundaries. But for now, I'm going to need time to practice these new skills, time to get used to taking on more responsibility and trusting my own decisions. As I feel more in charge of my life, I realize that I am having less anxiety and fewer panic attacks.

This is one of many stories that make their way to Open Door meetings. A woman, recently married, told the support group, "I feel as though I'll never make another decision or think for myself again." Whether this was true, or simply her perception, it was enough to trigger her anxiety and panic attacks. She went on to explain that her husband went ahead and made decisions without asking for her opinion. Hesitant to speak up and risk confrontation, she tried to ignore the fact that her feelings were being discounted. But doing so only made her feel resentful.

We need to know that our opinions count. Sooner or later we see how the lack of assertiveness and the inability to take the initiative can affect our self-esteem and make it difficult to maintain a balanced relationship. Feeling helpless and lacking control of our lives, we struggle to regain some of our independence.

Becoming More Assertive

Nonassertiveness isn't necessarily a consistent behavior. We might find it easier to express how we feel, or to ask for what we need, when dealing with someone we trust. But with someone who is hostile or easily takes offense, we might weigh the odds, keep our feelings to ourselves and protect our self-esteem. Sometimes it is best to hold back. And yet, in a relationship or work environment, a complete breakdown in communication could result if issues go unresolved and resentment builds. We might give up if we feel powerless and unable to bring about any change.

However, we can learn to become more assertive through an assertiveness training class or professional counseling. To increase awareness, we can read self-help books on the subject. Practicing on our own, we might begin by expressing our feelings or opinions in situations that are nonthreatening, with people we trust. It may help to reassure ourselves that we have the right to express them.

Establishing Boundaries

Developing assertiveness can help with establishing boundaries. We find it difficult to speak up for ourselves because of our overabundant need for approval, our fear of criticism or rejection, and the possibility of confrontation. At times we're not sure when our boundaries are being crossed. This is especially true if we have come from a dysfunctional background. It is difficult to know what is normal and where to draw the line. Self-doubt meets us at every turn.

Establishing boundaries means knowing when to say *no* rather than taking on more than we can handle. It means becoming more assertive in our relationships or work environment. This is not an easy task for those of us who seldom disagree, or have a difficult time expressing our feelings or opinions.

In the following story, we see how Mara's inability to assert herself and take charge in the workplace contributes to her anxiety.

Mara's Story

A colleague and I were trying to work through a crisis at the office. Just before we were about to confront those involved, she told me that she would handle the matter on her own—and then just walked away. I stood there, stunned. I felt as though I no longer had any say in the matter. The message I got was: You're not capable of handling this so I'll take care of it myself. No sooner had the door closed behind her when I felt the panic building. A rush of adrenaline left me feeling out of control.

Episodes like this had happened before. Though I had seniority, my colleague would sometimes just take over and run the show. Rather than speak up and take the chance of rocking the boat, I stuffed my feelings and went with the flow. I tried hard to convince myself that the issue wasn't worth it. That is, until I realized what it was doing to my self-esteem and how it was feeding into my anxiety and panic attacks.

Dealing With Confrontation

We avoid confrontation at all costs. Perhaps we feel there is no way we can win. Rather than feel further loss of self-esteem, we figure it's better to avoid the situation altogether. However, not coming to our own defense or speaking our mind can leave us feeling helpless. Not meeting conflict head-on can feel debilitating because we feel that we're unable to cope. But rather than being hard on ourselves for avoiding confrontation, we might want to take time to reflect on what we've had to deal with in our lives. Why wouldn't helplessness be a familiar feeling for us? Many of us grew up in circumstances we couldn't change. We felt powerless. How could we have learned assertiveness? We knew that it was best to tough it out and not complain. Coming to our own defense was not acceptable. In order to keep the peace we had to pull together as a family, often in silence.

Denial, avoidance, and minimizing are coping strategies that many of us learned when we were young. If we lived in a dysfunctional environment, for example, these strategies worked for us. They got us through difficult times. Unfortunately, when we moved out into the adult world, we brought these same coping strategies with us. It will take time to undo what we've been conditioned to do. However, we can let go of the past and learn new and healthier ways of dealing with our problems.

Moving Into a New Comfort Zone

We have looked at the problem of low self-esteem and the role it plays in our anxiety or panic attacks. We have talked about how we often compare ourselves with others, such as friends, acquaintances, or colleagues in the workplace. We may think that the other person is smarter, more talented, better organized, or more successful. Feeling inadequate, we often go the extra mile to make up for what we think we lack. In the process, we exhaust ourselves and discover that we just can't do enough to make up for that feeling of inadequacy. We need to find a way to recognize our strong points, allow for limitations, and be more accepting of ourselves. By doing this, we may find ourselves moving into a new comfort zone.

The following story is an example of how I came to realize my strengths, and at the same time, accept of my limitations.

Judy's Story

The breakthrough for me on self-acceptance came when I took a written test at a teachers' workshop that revealed one's personal characteristics and learning style. The information clearly showed my strengths as well as my limitations. I learned that whatever I lacked was made up for with any number of strong points. For example, though I am not detail-oriented nor am I as well organized as some of my colleagues, I am sensitive, empathetic and people-oriented. Even though logic isn't one of my attributes, I am imaginative, creative and artistic. What made this test so important to me was that I liked the person I was seeing. It was as though I had moved into a whole new comfort zone. I no longer needed to compare or make excuses for what I felt I lacked.

When we understand ourselves better, we can appreciate our qualities, which we often overlook or take for granted, and we can be more accepting of what we consider to be our shortcomings. We take a major step in our recovery when we learn to accept who we are, when we can be ourselves and not who we think we should be.

Points to remember: *Growing in Awareness*

1. It helps to become aware of what lies beneath our anxiety or panic attacks. They are there for a reason. They are trying to tell us something.

2. Gaining an awareness of, and expressing, our feelings, is an essential part of recovery.

3. We can begin practicing assertiveness by expressing our feelings in situations that are non-threatening, with people we trust.

4. Developing assertiveness can help with establishing boundaries in our relationships and work environment.

5. Although denial, avoidance, and minimization were coping strategies for some of us when we were young, we can let go of the past and learn new and healthier ways of dealing with our problems.

6. When we understand ourselves better, we can appreciate our qualities, which we often overlook, and can be more accepting of what we consider to be our shortcomings.

7. We take a major step in our recovery when we accept who we are and not try to become who we think we should be.

CHAPTER FIVE

AWARENESS THROUGH JOURNALING

*As time goes on, I find that I'm more open
about my feelings. And I'm beginning to realize
the importance of sharing them. It's one of
the many risks I've been taking.*

*Journal entry
March, 1984*

AWARENESS THROUGH JOURNALING

It is difficult to believe that I was ever at such a low point in my life.
Through journaling I can see how far I've come in my recovery

We get so caught up in our anxiety, unpredictable panic attacks, self-imposed time limits and setbacks, that we're not always aware of our progress. As a result, we may feel helpless, frustrated and discouraged. Journal writing, however, is one way to raise our awareness and break through the frustration. By keeping an ongoing record, we can track our progress. Despite inevitable setbacks and plateaus, we can clearly see our successes, no matter how small.

Journaling can take various forms. We can keep a diary to record our symptoms, self-talk and other coping strategies. Especially when dealing with challenging situations. We can use unsent letters or poetry to express our thoughts or vent our feelings.

Regardless of form, journaling can help us through many of life's experiences. It can have a positive effect on us, both physically and emotionally. According to James J. Pennebaker, professor of psychology at the University of Texas at Austin, writing about our experiences—especially the difficult ones—can help strengthen the immune system and lower blood pressure.[33] Because journaling can help in the healing process, it has been prescribed by both doctors and therapists.

In this chapter we will discuss the different ways to journal and discover what we can learn from our writing.

How to Journal

Recording how we deal with challenging situations

In addition to anxiety symptoms, self-talk and other coping strategies, we can record how we deal with situations that are particularly challenging for us. For example, travel. I wrote the following journal entries during a trip that my family and I made to Chicago. It seemed like an impossible venture since I was in a setback. However, I wanted to attend a special event in the Chicago area despite having to ride in a car for six hours. Though I knew it would be difficult I was willing to take the risk. Although written in 1983, these journal entries will sound very familiar, since I was learning the strategies used in this book. I might add that it isn't necessary to write so many entries at one time.

Saturday

5:30 a.m.—Left for Chicago. Stomach upset, headache, and a lot of anxiety. Didn't expect to feel miserable in my own driveway. I have a long road ahead of me. Not sure I'll be able to

---

33 Tibbetts, Tammy. "The Joys of Journaling," Ladies Home Journal, page 12, August, 2007.

stay in control during the whole trip. Trying to accept how I'm feeling. That's all it is, a feeling. I'm not in any danger.

6:00 a.m.—Tried lying down. Thought it might help my anxiety, but it didn't work.

6:20 a.m.—Decided to sit up and get in touch with my surroundings. Distraction wasn't helping, so I'm trying to be okay with my anxiety. Giving myself reasons for why I'm feeling the way I do. I've had a tense week. Past experience with travel has been difficult and it's my first time taking a trip in quite a while.

6:50 a.m.—Still allowing for the possibility of a panic attack. Staying in the present, getting involved in conversation, and taking in the scenery helps. Anxiety is starting to settle down.

8:00 a.m.—Stopped for breakfast. I didn't rush, but stayed in the present. Back in the car I'm feeling the same anticipation as before. I feel stranded on a highway far away from home. Trying to keep my expectations low and allow myself to be anxious. I can get out of the car and walk around if necessary. Continuing to allow any symptoms.

11:30 a.m.—My mind is rushing. I'm trying to stay in the present but my inner dialogue vacillates between acceptance and nonacceptance. What if I panic? Who cares! Just go ahead and panic! Is it always going to be this way? Embrace the fear. Have I failed in some way? It's okay to fail! I keep reminding myself that, considering the tremendous risk I'm taking, there's no way I can fail. It's taking a lot of courage to make this trip.

12:35 p.m.—Feeling good about how things are going, but tired and stiff from sitting. Continuing to keep my expectations low.

2:30 p.m.—Arrived in Chicago. Had worried about being in a lot of traffic, but so far, no problem. I feel so much a part of life. Planning to stop at the Chicago Art Institute. I can't believe I'm doing this. It's wonderful!

5:30 p.m.—Checked into the hotel. Exhausted! While at the Art Institute, my mind started to rush. Felt dizzy, light-headed. Tried to slow down, focus on the present, and allow the dizziness. It worked! I seemed to feel more centered.

Sunday
4:00 p.m.—Had a panic attack when we arrived at the reception. I just let it happen without attaching any danger. Tried to float through it. Anxiety continued. Kept lowering my expectations. Felt very emotional. Kept tearing up. Fear of losing control. Continued to lower my expectations. Allowed for all my feelings. The anxiety eventually let up.

In looking back over these entries I was able to assess how I handled each phase of the trip. I could see a familiar pattern in my coping strategies, such as focusing on the present, slowing down, using a self-talk that allowed for any anxiety symptoms. I could see what worked and what didn't work.

In my first entry at 5:30 a.m. I was concerned about staying in control during the long road ahead. I was putting the trip into a time frame by focusing on how long it would take before we arrived in Chicago. This awareness of time and distance between my "safe place" and my destination only added to the anticipatory anxiety. It would have helped to focus on the present, rather than on the entire trip at once.

Afraid of losing control, I tried pretending to be somewhere else, such as in the safety of my home. However, that did not prove to be an effective strategy. The anxiety didn't start to decrease until I paid attention to my surroundings. Then I was more permissive of my anxiety symptoms and used a self-talk that reassured me that I was not in any danger. I gave myself a simple explanation of why I was anxious. These steps were far more effective than trying hard to stay in control or trying to distract myself from my feelings.

Stopping for any reason when traveling was always difficult for me. I would rather have driven straight through just to get the trip over with as quickly as possible. When we did stop for breakfast, however, I tried to stay in the present and allow for any anxiety I might experience. I told myself that if I felt panicky, I could always go back out to the car. I tried to reassure myself that I was safe, that nothing was going to happen to me even if I felt anxious. As always, acceptance was the key.

When we arrived at the reception, I found myself in the throes of a panic attack. It is not unusual to experience anxiety or panic after the worst is over and we least expect it. What helped me the most during the attack was once again lowering my expectations and allowing for whatever might happen. By not building up a resistance, the anxiety did eventually subside.

Returning home from the trip, I experienced a great feeling of accomplishment. Needless to say, we can gain confidence by taking such risks. Today it is difficult to believe that anxiety had such a hold on me, but through journaling, I can see how far I've come in my recovery. I've made a number of trips across the country since my Chicago venture without giving it a second thought. Recovery is possible!

Recording Our Progress

While in therapy, Marion kept a journal where she recorded her panic attacks and the strategies she used in dealing with them. The awareness she gained proved a valuable asset. Not only was she able to chart her progress, as erratic as it was, but she could share the important data with her therapist and ask specific questions.

When this journal was written, Marion had been in therapy for almost seven months and was already seeing her anxiety in a different light. Her supportive and permissive self-talk was making a difference in how she dealt with her panic attacks. She no longer saw herself as a victim, and was taking the steps necessary to move forward in her recovery.

The following is a week's worth of entries:

Tuesday—*I'm going through a period of high stress at work. Rather than avoiding conflict, I've been trying to be more assertive and face some of the problems head on.*

Wednesday—*I've really been pushing myself at the office, which leaves me depleted and makes my weekends difficult to deal with. This past weekend I tried telling myself that it was okay to be tired and gave myself permission to take it easy. As it turned out, the weekend went pretty well. I was able to channel the little energy I had into some leisure activities.*

Thursday—*I experienced a panic attack during a staff meeting, but handled it well. I first asked myself why. But I told myself to accept what it was, to embrace the fear rather than fight it. I knew I could get up and leave if I had to. Using this self-talk, I was able to stay. I had another attack while driving home. My thoughts were racing, so I focused on slowing down and going with the feeling.*

Saturday—*I spent 4 hours at the mall with little or no problem. I told myself that there was no hurry and that I could leave at any time. While I was there I could feel the difference between rushing and slowing down. I was also aware that my mind still had a tendency to rush even though my body had slowed down.*

Sunday—*Drove to the library. I was feeling weak and dizzy before I left home, so I kept my expectations low. Had a panic attack on the way. I was pretty shaken, but told myself I could turn back at any time. The symptoms continued while I was there. After 30 minutes I decided to leave. I tried not to see my leaving as failure. I was disappointed because I wanted to stay longer. My biggest problem was the dizziness. I feel like my anxiety is going to last forever, which really scares me. I don't want to live this way.*

Monday—*It's difficult for me to go out when I'm not feeling well, which is often the case. On days when I'm feeling okay I don't think about panicking. On days when I'm not feeling well I try to reassure myself that there is nothing seriously wrong, that my symptoms are caused by stress. I then try to keep my expectations low and allow for whatever happens.*

By journaling between sessions Marion could take a close look at her self-talk, the risks she was taking, and the stressors that fed into her anxiety.

In her entry for Sunday, she noted how disturbed she was by the chronic dizziness and expressed hopelessness. When we think there's no way out, we can feel helpless to the point of despair. This is a frightening and serious thought, but not uncommon. Despite such thoughts, all is not lost. We can move beyond them.

Even though Marion's panic attacks appeared erratic, she was able to make a connection, attributing them to high stress at work, fatigue, and feeling rushed. Making a connection is important, since we can become very discouraged when all seems to be going well and suddenly the panic or anxiety resurfaces. Acceptance, low expectations, and slowing down were important strategies that contributed to her progress.

Recording Our Feelings

In chapter 4, *Growing in Awareness*, we learned that gaining awareness of our feelings and expressing them are essential to the recovery process. Journal writing can help. It is a safe place to vent our feelings and it can yield insights into the source of our anxiety problem. For example, feelings of loneliness and isolation are prominent in the following excerpt from my journal. Whether actual or perceived, these emotions were a definite link to my panic attacks, and gave evidence of an underlying depression, which often accompanies anxiety.

Everything has become so hazy, so muddled. I've even grown numb to the numbness. If I could just cry. I really think I could if I allowed myself to do so. However, it would be done as if in a vacuum. I feel so cut off...so isolated. Who am I now? Sometimes adrift, sometimes with great purpose and determination, always lonely. Sometimes the aloneness is comfortable, almost refreshing and renewing. Other times it is paralyzing.

When we see the same feelings surface time and time again in our journal, we become aware of what might be triggering our anxiety and panic attacks and what keeps them recurring. Through my journaling, I got to a point where I could actually predict an attack based on how I was feeling or what I was thinking.

Everything appearing *hazy and muddled,* for example, might suggest that I was avoiding the heart of my problem. Growing *numb to the numbness* could mean that I was in denial, a safe and comfortable place in which to hide. Facing the central issues could mean having to make changes—a risky, frightening prospect, especially given our vulnerability. In the following story, Susan writes about getting in touch with her emotions through journaling and how it helped her deal with a family crisis.

Susan's Story

In the spring of 1993 I started on a path that was to take me to a wondrous place of self-exploration. I enrolled in a fantastic journaling class through adult education with the most compassionate teacher I have ever had the pleasure to learn from. I took it for four semesters and during that time a miracle occurred. I learned to get in touch with my feelings through journaling. Now I truly know how freeing and healing journal writing can be. I am a convert.

Years before, when my therapist wanted me to talk to my agoraphobia, I obviously would have been talking to myself. I was the only one who knew what was standing in my way, which was the point of the exercise. We all have the answers to most of our problems inside us. We just have to learn ways to bring them out. Journaling is one way of doing this.

Finding our emotions and working on them in this safe way is a powerful "life tool." During the class, I had to deal with a family crisis. Instead of overreacting as I might have done in the past, I wrote about my feelings and worked out ways to get myself through this rough time. I weathered the storm at least 80 percent better than I would have if I had not been journaling.

Writing Unsent Letters

Losing a loved one is devastating. The finality of death can leave us feeling helpless, alone, and empty. But in spite of caring family and friends, we can't always share our innermost thoughts with them.

Six months after my mother died it seemed like there was no one left to turn to. Each time I tried to talk about my deep loss, I would get a look that chided: Are you still dealing with that? Or people would ask: Have you thought about seeing a therapist? Finally, I decided to write out my feelings in a journal, a process that lasted seven years. Each entry was in the form of a letter, in which I told my mother about the day's happenings and about our family. I reminisced about all the good times she and I had had together. More important, I was able to tell her how much I missed her and what a difficult time I was having without her. Alone with my journal, I could remember the good times, as well as pour my heart out in grief.

There are other reasons for writing letters. It could be to a friend who has moved away, or someone who lives nearby. It could be a letter to a significant other. Perhaps there was a misunderstanding and we want to tell them how we feel. It could be an expression of anger or regret, or a letter of forgiveness. Those of us who have a difficult time expressing our feelings can benefit from this form of writing. Since these letters are not sent to the person they're addressed to, there is no possibility of confrontation, criticism, or rejection.

Writing Prose and Poetry

In addition to letters, we can express our feelings through poetry. Without trying to write the perfect poem, we simply write down words that express our thoughts and feelings. Then, without concern about rhyme or meter, we simply arrange them in a meaningful order. We do not have to see ourselves as poets to express ourselves through poetry. It's just another form of writing.

My mother died suddenly. The anger and shock I experienced is evident in the following verse.

I feel as though a light has gone out.
With great effort I move from day to day
trying hard to recall the sound of your voice,

fearing that my memory will fail me.
A silent rage rises within me.
In desperation I search for answers.
Whose "great plan" is this?

Expressing these feelings in writing gave a sense of release. Over time, I was able to let go of them.

When my husband died, I grieved in simple prose. I wrote an account of our last days together and described milestones I wanted to remember and share with my family. I recorded conversations that I was continuing to have with him. I wrote to vent feelings, so deep and intense, often through tears. My writing helped sustain me during those first years of widowhood.

Writing can also help with troubling thoughts or feelings. On-going feelings that hover on the edge of obsession. By exploring them through writing, we can discover their meaning. By expressing them in a journal, we may discover why we continue to harbor them and over time release them.

Hold on to this feeling...treasure its existence
for it has become a part of you.
It breathes life into your everyday existence,
sustains you, and brings light into the gray areas
of your life.
You gave birth to it in a time of need.
It nurtured you through long hours of loneliness.

Keeping a journal—whether in the form of diary, letters, prose, or poetry—serves many purposes. We see how repressed feelings play a significant role in our anxiety problem and realize the benefits of expressing them. We discover how the stressful events in our lives contribute to our anxiety or panic attacks, and become more aware of the self-talk and other coping strategies that work for us. We look back and reflect on where we've been and how far we've come in our recovery. Journaling gives us written testimony that we are, indeed, making progress.

Points to Remember: *Journaling*

1. Journal writing can take various forms, such as a diary, letters, prose, or poetry.

2. Journaling promotes and develops awareness of feelings. It is an effective and safe way for us to express them.

3. Through our writing, we can gain insights into the source of our anxiety problem. We can see how the stressful events in our lives contribute to our anxiety or panic attacks.

4. In our journal, we can record risks we've taken and how we've managed them.

5. By recording our self-talk, and other coping strategies, we can see how they help us deal with our anxiety or panic attacks.

6. Writing an unsent letter is a safe way to express our feelings since there is no possibility of confrontation, criticism, or rejection.

7. Through journaling, we can follow the progress we are making and see how far we've come in our recovery.

CHAPTER SIX

BEYOND ACCEPTANCE

*One of the things I've noticed about my yoga class is that
I have a sense of calm at the end of each session.
I'm actually able to shop and run errands
after class because I feel less anxious.*

Journal entry
August, 1975

QUESTIONS ON SELF-CARE

Physical health and a sense of personal wellness, vitality, and robustness comprise one of the most important foundations of self-esteem
—Edmund J. Bourne[34]

Although the *Power of Acceptance* is based on a cognitive program, the strategies and self-talk are only part of the total picture in dealing with anxiety and panic attacks. Taking care of ourselves is important in achieving and maintaining better health, both mental and physical. Although brief, I include this section on self-care because:

- We are good caregivers, but we often neglect our own need for exercise, proper rest, and relaxation.
- We are sensitive to physical symptoms of any kind. When we aren't feeling well, it is difficult to go out and take the risks that are necessary for our recovery. Maintaining good health can only be to our advantage.
- Exercise and taking time to relax can help us better handle stress.

---

34 Bourne, *Anxiety & Phobia Workbook,* page 317.

- People often come to support group meetings with questions about self-care: How do I get started on an exercise program? What types of exercise are helpful? Will exercise bring on anxiety or panic symptoms? What can I do about insomnia? Is there a nutritional supplement that will help? Is diaphragmatic breathing helpful? Why don't relaxation exercises always work for me? What about meditation? What is biofeedback?

How do I get started on an exercise program?
Getting started can be the most difficult part of an exercise program. Just thinking about making time in a busy schedule can be discouraging. It helps to have reasonable expectations. For example, we might start by planning to walk for fifteen minutes at least three times per week. If that sounds like it's hardly worth the effort, keep in mind that doing any kind of exercise is good, and walking for fifteen minutes makes it easier to walk for twenty minutes. Whatever exercise we choose, it is a good idea to keep it simple and begin slowly. If we have a hard time getting motivated to exercise on our own, we can sign up for an exercise class through the YMCA, a local health club, or community education.

Will exercise bring on anxiety symptoms?
Many of us are concerned about having anxiety or a panic attack while exercising. It is possible to experience such physical symptoms as light-headedness or heart palpitations. They can be very

disturbing, but as you know, are not harmful. The benefits of exercise far outweigh any temporary discomfort we might experience. However, it is advisable to check with your doctor before beginning any kind of exercise program. If you are concerned about having physical symptoms, gentle stretching or yoga might be a good alternative to more strenuous forms of exercise, such as aerobics.

I enrolled in a yoga class before I knew I was dealing with a panic disorder. After stretching, relaxing, and meditating for an hour and a half I noticed a calmness that stayed with me for several hours. Since I was having a difficult time going into stores because of my panic attacks, I decided to do my shopping after each class and was able to do so with little or no anxiety.

What types of exercise are helpful?
There are many different types of exercise: walking, jogging, biking, and swimming. The list goes on. All can be helpful. It's mostly a matter of preference. Choosing something we enjoy will make it easier to work an exercise program into our schedule. It will also help keep up the routine. I prefer a brisk walk, water aerobics, or yoga. I find that these types of exercise help to energize me. They also relieve my anxiety when I am under stress. Although exercise can reduce muscle tension and stimulate the production of endorphins (which contributes to a sense of well-being), I do not consider an exercise program to be the answer to overcoming intense anxiety and panic attacks. I was convinced of this when two marathon runners attended an Open Door meeting on the same night.

While exercise is no cure-all, it is definitely a plus for our overall health and well-being. It can help us handle stress more effectively. Feeling good physically is good for anyone, especially anxiety sufferers who often feel tired and depressed, and spend a great deal of time worrying about their health in general.

Are there nutritional supplements that might help my anxiety?
I took a yoga class in 1985. Our instructor encouraged us to consider taking vitamins B and C, and calcium-magnesium as nutritional supplements. She explained that under stress our body becomes depleted of the B and C vitamins. She went on to say that calcium-magnesium is known as a natural tranquilizer. Wanting to find some relief from my anxiety, I took these supplements religiously for many years. I later found these very same supplements mentioned in Bourne's *Anxiety and Phobia Workbook*,[35] along with an excellent, in-depth chapter on nutrition.

What can I do about insomnia?
It is not uncommon for those of us with anxiety to have difficulty sleeping. (Chronic insomnia is experienced by 10 to 33 percent of adults in the United States.[36]) Not getting a good night's sleep is especially frustrating for us because it can aggravate our anxiety.

---

35 Bourne, *Anxiety & Phobia Workbook,* page 346.
36 Gardner, James and Arthur H. Bell. *Overcoming Anxiety, Panic & Depression: New Ways to Regain Your Confidence.* Franklin Lakes, NJ: The Career Press, Inc., 2000. page 188.

I have found the following suggestions helpful in maintaining a normal sleep pattern:

- Because drinking anything caffeinated late in the day interferes with my sleep, I switch to decaffeinated beverages mid-afternoon. This fits into the suggested six-hour timeframe for avoiding caffeine before bedtime.[37] For those of us who are caffeine-sensitive, it's a good idea to avoid coffee, tea, colas, and other such stimulants altogether. In some people with panic disorder, coffee can actually trigger panic attacks.[38]

- I try to stay on a regular schedule by going to bed and getting up at the same time each day. The body has its own natural rhythms of wakefulness and sleepiness. An irregular sleep–wake cycle can throw those rhythms out of balance.[39]

- To help me relax before going to bed, a light snack has become part of my bedtime routine. Another part of that routine is reading. No mysteries or thrillers, but something low-key and calming. Since exercising too close to bedtime can have an adverse effect, I do gentle stretching.

- If I find myself tossing and turning in bed, I get up and

---

37 Gardner and Bell, *Overcoming Anxiety, Panic & Depression,* page 189.
38 Peurifoy, Reneau Z. *Anxiety, Phobias, & Panic: A Step-by-Step Program for Regaining Control of Your Life.* New York: Warner Books, 1995. page 60.
39 Montgomery, Bob and Laurel Morris. *Living With Anxiety: A Clinically Tested Step-by-Step Plan for Drug-Free Management.* Cambridge, Mass.: Perseus Publishing, 2001. page 194.

move around for a while, continuing to read or watch television until I'm sleepy. I then return to bed.

- When we are anxious, our thoughts run rampant. In addition to mulling over the problems of the day, we worry about not getting enough sleep. (I turn my clock to the wall so that I'm not tempted to look at it during the night.) We tell ourselves, *I have to get some sleep tonight because tomorrow is a big day*, or *If I don't fall asleep soon I'll be exhausted tomorrow*. The more we give ourselves these messages, the harder it is to fall asleep. Instead, we might say, *Even if I can't sleep tonight, I can still rest. I will be able to sleep eventually. The worst that will happen is I'll be tired tomorrow. But I will be able to function in spite of how I'm feeling*. More than once, I've surprised myself with the amount of energy I've had after only four hours of sleep.

- If nothing seems to work we may obsess about our lack of sleep. Then we're dealing with an even bigger problem. We may find ourselves dreading going to bed for fear we will have a repeat performance of tossing and turning. If insomnia becomes a chronic problem, it is advisable to consult a doctor.

Is diaphragmatic breathing helpful?

Diaphragmatic breathing (deep breathing from the diaphragm) is recommended for those of us dealing with anxiety and panic attacks because we chronically hyperventilate and thus create an imbalance in the body's oxygen and carbon dioxide levels. By slowing down our breathing we reduce the oxygen intake, bringing the ratio of oxygen to carbon dioxide back into balance.[40]

I have found this breathing technique helpful before public speaking, during performances at school, in a crisis, or when feeling stressed. However, it was not effective when caught up in a panic attack. I found it difficult to focus on anything—including my breathing—and ended up holding my breath altogether.

If diaphragmatic breathing doesn't help, we need to be okay with that and not think we're doing something wrong. This technique might be more challenging for someone in the early stages of an anxiety disorder, but useful later on with a better understanding of a panic attack's physiological processes. Again, different methods work for different people, and it's important to find out what works for us.

Why don't relaxation exercises always work for me?
Many people who come to the Open Door support groups feel they have failed with any number of relaxation exercises, and thus failed at what they see as a simple solution to their problem. But much depends on the approach to relaxation. It is possible that we are trying too hard. The *I have to relax* attitude can have the opposite effect. If we don't get immediate results we wonder why the relaxation exercises aren't working and become discouraged.

---

40 Bourne, *Anxiety & Phobia Workbook,* page 70.

For those of us with an anxiety disorder, *control* is a big issue. We are constantly on guard, worrying about the sudden onset of anxiety or panic. This makes it difficult to let go and relax. If this happens, it is a good idea to start out slowly, adding time to our relaxation sessions. Perseverance will eventually pay off. While achieving a state of relaxation isn't the total solution to our problem, it is an important part of anxiety and stress management.

What about meditation?

Some people associate meditation with religion or a particular culture. But meditation is practiced all over the world regardless of religion. Anyone can benefit from it. It can be a spiritual experience or it can simply be an exercise in calming the mind. Sitting in a comfortable position, in a quiet place, we focus on our (diaphragmatic) breathing. Going within, we allow ourselves to just "be." As we meditate, thoughts may continue to distract us. Without being disturbed by them, we simply allow them to pass through our consciousness. When the mind is calm or centered, we experience a detachment from our problems and concerns.

The practice of meditation offers both emotional and physical advantages. It can help us achieve a state of relaxation and an increase in mental awareness; it can decrease heart rate, respiration rate, and blood pressure.[41]

---

41 Wilson, *Don't Panic,* page 166.

What is biofeedback?

In biofeedback an electronic device detects the body's physiological responses, such as muscle tension and breathing patterns. Any change in them is conveyed to the user by way of a monitor. Biofeedback thus shows how our thoughts and feelings affect our muscle tension and breathing patterns. The idea is that through this awareness, we will have greater control over our physiological responses and will be able to change negative responses into more positive ones.

In my own biofeedback training, I worked on my fear of flying, and visualized myself boarding a jet airliner. As my imagination reached takeoff, I was amazed to see the pointer steadily advance. Just thinking about flying had raised my tension level.

Points to Remember: *Self-Care*

1. We are good caregivers, but we often neglect our own need for exercise, proper rest, and relaxation.

2. Exercise is a plus for our overall health and well-being. It can help us handle stress more effectively.

3. When exercising, it is possible to experience such physical symptoms as light-headedness or heart palpitations, though they are not necessarily harmful.

4. It is always advisable to check with a doctor before beginning any kind of exercise program.

5. Insomnia is not uncommon for those of us with anxiety. Staying on a regular sleep schedule, avoiding caffeine, and using a helpful

self-talk are a few useful strategies.

6. Diaphragmatic breathing is recommended for those of us with an anxiety disorder because we tend to chronically hyperventilate.

7. Meditation can be a spiritual experience or simply an exercise in calming the mind. Everyone can benefit from it.

8. Through biofeedback we can see how our thoughts and feelings affect our muscle tension and breathing patterns.

THOUGHTS ON MEDICATION

*Even when we take medication, we need to give
ourselves credit for the progress we're making*

Questions about medication often come up at Open Door meetings. In fact, the subject of prescription drugs could easily dominate any group discussion. For this reason, I have included the following information, which is strictly from the layperson's viewpoint. Unless footnoted, it is based on my own experience and observations. It is not meant as a recommendation one way or the other about taking or not taking medication. That decision must be made under the guidance of a medical doctor or professional therapist.

The focus of this chapter is on our *thoughts* about taking prescription drugs. It answers questions such as, "How do we know when medication is the right choice?" and "What problems might be encountered?" Medication is a topic of concern because drugs are often perceived as a quick and simple solution to a complex problem. On the other hand, there may be some concern about side effects, or the possibility of becoming dependent on medication.

Should I or shouldn't I?

People who attend Open Door meetings are divided on the question of medication. Some take it, some do not. Not all persons with anxiety need medication. What is important to stress is that *recovery is possible either way.*

The question becomes pressing when someone in the group has shared their success with a particular prescription drug. And yet, what works for one person doesn't necessarily work for the next. Everyone is different. But hope springs eternal, and the possibility of finding relief from anxiety continues to raise the question, *Should I or shouldn't I?*

How do we know when medication is the right choice?

According to Edmund Bourne two factors influence whether medication should be used. The first is severity. When panic attacks, obsessions and compulsions, or depressive symptoms are severe enough to prevent one from performing ordinary activities, or when symptoms have reached the point where just getting through each day is a struggle, medication may be helpful. The second factor is personal values. Some anxiety sufferers feel a commitment to recover by natural means.[42] Before relying on medication, Bourne suggests exploring natural methods.

---

42 Bourne, *Anxiety & Phobia Workbook,* pages 361 & 362.

My doctor recommends medication but I'm afraid to try it

Many of us who deal with an anxiety problem are phobic about taking medication. We're afraid that the side effects might make us feel even more out of control. It is true that certain medications can have side effects that resemble the very symptoms we are trying to alleviate.[43] Not knowing which symptoms are caused by anxiety and which ones are caused by the medication can be confusing. If the side effects are anxiety-producing, we feel there's no relief.

Another reason for concern is that we want to be in control of handling our anxiety or panic attacks. We may see our dependence on medication as long-term. More than one person in group has commented, "I don't want to spend the rest of my life on medication."

If medication is advised and we're afraid to take it, we can discuss our fears with our doctor or therapist. Our self-talk can also help with some reassurance. For example, we might say to ourselves, *Even if I don't like the idea of taking medication, I'll do what I need to do for now. I will be able to manage my anxiety on my own when I'm ready.*

What if I take medication and it doesn't work?

I remember thinking of taking medication as a last resort. I was actually afraid to try it because I might discover that it wasn't effective. If that were to happen, it would leave me with no options. Just

---

43 Beckfield, *Master Your Panic,* page 167.

knowing there was something out there that *might* relieve some of my anxiety was enough to help remove a feeling of hopelessness.

Taking medication does not guarantee results. However, the fact that a particular medication isn't working doesn't mean we have failed in any way or that there is something wrong with us. Different prescription drugs work for different people. If we're not getting the results we want, it is a good idea to consult our doctor or therapist.

According to Denise Beckfield, when taking antidepressants for panic, we need to be on the medication for several weeks before receiving full benefit from it. Perhaps even several months, before we achieve the maximal benefit from the medication.[44]

I'm afraid I'll become dependent on medication

Many of us fear becoming psychologically dependent on a prescribed drug. We can also feel vulnerable when decisions about medication are in someone else's hands, such as the length of time it is prescribed. Some of us worry about our medication suddenly being terminated. Although this would not happen with medication prescribed for anxiety/depression, these thoughts may occur. It's an issue of control. Someone else is making decisions about a medication that we have come to rely on.

Carol's Story

I went to pick up my medication at the pharmacy and found

---

44 Beckfield, *Master Your Panic,* pages 166 & 167.

out that my doctor had not phoned it in. Afraid of with-drawal symptoms, I called my doctor but was told he couldn't come to the phone. As my anxiety increased, I found myself shouting, "I need to talk to my doctor now!" I was out of control. As I left the pharmacy, embarrassed, I made a deci-sion. I never wanted anything (or anyone) to have that kind of control over me again. I promptly found a new physician who would help me get off my meds. I was ready to make that decision, since my therapist had given me effective tools to work with. Within a year, I was medication-free.

I'm afraid to go off or change my medication

Many of us want to get off medication eventually, but view the prospect with apprehension. Even if we're not getting the results we want, we may persist in taking a prescribed drug with the thought, *If I'm having a difficult time now, how much worse would it be if I were to go off of my medication altogether?* We may also react with alarm when our doctor or therapist suggests trying a different medication from the one that we are taking. We might think that even if our current prescription is not as effective as we want it to be, we at least know what to expect from it. Any kind of change is unsettling.

Another fear is having a setback. We are afraid that by discon-tinuing our medication, the anxiety or panic attacks will recur. If medication is the only treatment used, there is a chance of that happening. But if medication is taken in conjunction with other methods, such as cognitive-behavioral therapy, we are learning strategies that will prepare us to cope with the anxiety on our own.[45] Our therapist will know when we are ready to go off medication. At that point, it will be a mutual decision. A tapering off period will allow time to detect a possible setback.

What problems might I encounter when taking medication?
It has been my experience, and observation, that when we take medication we can lose confidence in our own ability to cope with anxiety or panic attacks. For example, when we do well in handling a difficult situation, such as driving on the highway or attending a social function, we tend to give all the credit to the medication. One case in particular comes to mind. A member of our support group announced, "I'm really doing much better. I've been taking my medication for a year now and it's finally taking effect." There was no mention of the coping strategies for anxiety and helpful self-talk that she had learned over the past year. She discounted everything she had learned. We might feel more confident when taking medication, but we are the ones taking the risks and we need to give ourselves credit for our progress.

Another problem we might encounter has to do with how we feel about ourselves when we rely on a prescribed drug. For example, if we are giving ourselves the message that we should be able to handle our anxiety on our own, we are only going to cause ourselves

---

45 Beckfield, *Master Your Panic,* page 171.

more anxiety. Once again, acceptance comes into play. We need to be okay with whatever decision we make. Every so often I hear people say, "I'm able to drive now" or "I'm able to shop at the mall now," and then add almost apologetically, "But I'm on medication." There is no need to be apologetic. We would not feel the need to explain our taking a prescribed drug for a physical problem. What we are dealing with is equally difficult, and we do what we must to cope with our anxiety and get on with our lives.

I believe that a certain amount of discomfort is necessary when facing feared situations if we are to gain confidence in our coping skills. On the other hand, if we have a difficult time leaving the house or getting through the day because of anxiety or panic attacks, we might want to consider the options. Again, it is best to discuss this with a doctor or therapist.

Bev's Story

When I visited my doctor last fall I asked him to help me taper my medication. By reducing it very slowly I didn't notice that I was taking a lower dose. I was concerned that I wouldn't be able to do it. I gave myself lots of time and plenty of permission. If it didn't work for me now, I could try again at a later date. This attitude helped me to wean myself off completely by the end of the year, a goal I had set (though not in stone). Too many "shoulds" make recovery nearly impossible. A bunch of little steps in recovery turns out to be one big step. I like how that feels.

As of January I stopped taking medication. I felt that it was time to try it on my own. When I was advised to take medication four years ago I fought it tooth and nail. I was not going to take drugs. I finally did give in to my doctor's recommendation (scared as I was), telling myself I would take it only until I felt more grounded. My belief is that if medication can help me to get through some rough times, help me to focus on my recovery, and in turn feel better about myself and my life, then taking medication is okay.

Points to Remember: *Medication*

1. We need to be okay with our decision to take or not take medication. It is an option that should be discussed with a doctor or therapist.

2. According to Edmund Bourne two factors influence whether medication should be used: severity and personal values. Some anxiety sufferers feel a commitment to recover by natural means.

3. If we are to gain confidence in our coping skills, a certain amount of discomfort is necessary when facing feared situations.

4. When taking a prescribed drug, we may lose confidence in our ability to cope with our anxiety. We may give all the credit to the medication. We need to be careful to avoid giving away our power.

5. We are hesitant to go off of our medication because we're afraid of a setback. However, if medication is taken in conjunction

with other methods, such as cognitive–behavioral therapy, we are better prepared to cope with the anxiety on our own.

6. Recovery is possible with or without medication.

PARTING THOUGHTS
RECOVERY

*My heart is light this morning. Even the late April snow hasn't
dampened my spirits. Breaking down walls and getting
in touch with one's feelings can certainly be a risk, but oh,
the rewards are great! There are days when I feel that
I'll actually get through this difficult period of my life.
When there's joy in the morning, night is easier to bear.*

Journal entry
April, 1984

DEFINING RECOVERY

*I no longer see myself as a helpless victim
trapped in an unending cycle of fear and panic*

I remember the first time I entered my therapist's office at Abbott-Northwestern Hospital's Behavioral Medicine Clinic. It was a sunny October afternoon. I had been to a number of therapists over the years and had nearly given up on finding the answers I was so desperately searching for. But this person came highly recommended. I was told that he himself had been agoraphobic, knew the terror of a panic attack firsthand, and had now recovered. During the next twelve months I would hang on his every word, placing my complete trust in him. I had not done this with any previous therapists. Despite years of experience or extensive credentials, one important component had always been missing: they hadn't tasted fear.

My heart was heavy but hopeful as I sat down across from him.

"I know what you're thinking," he said. "You're thinking that I can't help you."

I was caught off guard. Could he read my mind?

"You're right," I answered, "but you're my last hope. If you can't help me no one can."

I wanted to believe that it would be different this time, that the person sitting across from me would fix it. He would be the one to wave a magic wand and make the anxiety disappear. *Six months*, I thought. *In six months I should be better, now that I'm seeing someone who really understands this problem.*

Six months came and went and I was still struggling with anxiety symptoms. I still lived in fear of that next panic attack.

Finally, during one of our sessions I said to him, "I have to do this myself don't I?"

He nodded. It was an important awareness, but not very comforting. He would continue to guide me, but it was up to me to take the necessary steps that would eventually lead to my recovery. How frightening it was to realize that I was the one I had to rely on to get to the other side of my anxiety and panic. No one else could make it go away or fix it. Not even this person who, I had hoped, could perform the miracle.

As therapy progressed, my perception of the problem began to change. The panic attacks lost their mysteriousness. They were no longer the ogre that attacked from out of nowhere. And I was no longer seeing myself as a helpless victim trapped in an unending cycle of fear. I came to see that I had options. Pieces of the puzzle began falling into place.

Panic attacks have not troubled me for over twenty years. I no longer wake up in the morning and wonder whether I will panic today. My life doesn't revolve around the possibility of the next attack. I drive on the highway during rush hour, sit through car washes, wait at red lights in the left-hand turn lane, cross bridges, mingle in crowds, and travel without a problem.

This does not mean that I am completely free of anxiety. That would be unrealistic. It can still occur under stress. But the anxiety symptoms do not of themselves cause concern. They are no longer mysterious nor frightening. I simply remind myself that this is how I react in stressful situations. Nor am I concerned about the recurrence of panic attacks. I do not live in fear of it. I've been there before and I've learned effective coping skills. In the process I've also gained personal insights. And yet, while there is no comparison between where I was when I was struggling with panic attacks and where I am now, I still make it a point to keep my recovery open-ended.

I believe that *acceptance* is still the key to my recovery. Not only accepting my anxiety and panic attacks, but learning to accept myself as well. This is expressed in the following paragraph, which is taken from an article I wrote for the Open Door Newsletter:

I like who I am on days when I clean and polish and the house looks spotless. But I also like who I am when I leave my bed unmade and dishes on the sink because it's more important to read a book or write poetry. I like who I am when I'm organized and feeling like I really have it all together. But I also like who I am when I'm two weeks behind on balancing my checkbook or I can't find whatever it is I'm looking for. I like who I am when I assert myself and express how I'm feeling, rather than weighing every word for fear of rejection or criticism. But I also like who I am when I walk away from an issue because it's just not that important to me. What it all comes down to is lowered expectations, with few or no demands, because of a self-talk based on acceptance, regardless of who I am on any given day.

What a boost it is to our self-esteem when we like who we are, when we can embrace ourselves with acceptance.

We've learned that recovery means more than being free of anxiety and panic attacks. It means feeling self-confident, recognizing our strong points and accepting our limitations. Recovery also means being open to expressing our feelings, asserting ourselves and establishing boundaries when necessary. It means having a stronger self-esteem.

Remember that the strategies discussed in this book are the same ones that helped me achieve my own recovery. They can help you achieve recovery as well. Perhaps you are thinking, *Okay, so it worked for her. But how do I know it will work for me?* or *Her anxiety was different from mine. Mine is much worse!* Such thoughts are not unusual. As anxiety sufferers, we often compare ourselves with others and feel that we have the worst possible case. Feeling trapped in an ongoing cycle of fear, we have a difficult time believing that there is a way out, that we can ever be free of this problem.

I well remember feeling the same way. I, too, was convinced that it would never end. But it did. And it can end for you as well. On some days you will feel hopeful, on some you will be filled with doubt. But no matter how discouraged you might become, don't give up. Recovery is out there, regardless of how long it takes.

Conclusion

It is my hope that you now have a better understanding of your anxiety disorder and that you have found new and effective ways of coping with your anxiety or panic attacks. I hope you have been able to identify with some of the anxiety–panic triggers and underlying issues that often go unnoticed. Above all, I hope that *The Power of Acceptance* has given you the support you need to get you through this difficult time in your life, that it has left you with a more positive feeling about yourself, and has given you renewed hope for recovery.

I feel very fortunate to have had the opportunity to touch the lives of people who are trying so hard to meet the challenge of each new day, who struggle with chronic anxiety, or live in constant anticipation of that next panic attack. I know this suffering only too well. But I know in my heart that we are not victims. We can move forward in spite of our fear and frustration, and rise above the discouragement of setbacks. We *can* take charge of our lives again. Through the power of acceptance we can break through the anxiety–panic cycle, move on with our lives, and experience a freedom we never thought possible.

APPENDIX

Questions from the Support Person's Perspective

Bibliography

About the Author

QUESTIONS FROM
THE SUPPORT PERSON'S PERSPECTIVE

The person with a strong support system is fortunate because
support makes a significant difference in their progress

I n the preceding chapters we concentrated on the concerns of
the anxiety–panic sufferer. We now turn to the support person:
the significant other, family member, friend, or coworker. By answering their questions and addressing their concerns, they will
gain a better understanding of the paradoxes involved in dealing
with this problem, and be of greater help with less internal stress.

The process of recovery from an anxiety or panic disorder may
seem straightforward: logical strategies, rational self-talk, simply facing one's fear. But recovery is neither simple nor clear cut. Progress
is anything but linear. Plateaus and setbacks are unavoidable. They
require patience, persistence, and above all, *acceptance*.

In order for the support person to be supportive, he must also
embrace acceptance. If the anxiety sufferer is to learn a self-talk that
is nonjudgmental and supportive, then the support person must
also be nonjudgmental and supportive. The person with a strong
support system is fortunate indeed because support can make a
significant difference in their progress.

I just don't understand what this is all about!

First of all, as a support person, you are not expected to understand something you have never experienced. No matter how much you have read about anxiety and panic disorders, unless you have actually experienced a panic attack, and the overwhelming fear that accompanies it, you really cannot grasp its intensity. The same holds true for chronic anxiety. However, even without this understanding, you can help by showing compassion and an interest in understanding what the anxiety sufferer is dealing with. You can give her a sense of security by reassuring her that you believe that what she is experiencing is real, and that you are there for her when needed.

First, let's take a look at what happens during a panic attack. The anxiety sufferer experiences intense physical symptoms that often come without warning and for no apparent reason. Symptoms may include any combination of the following: light headedness, a tingling sensation, tightness in the chest, sweaty palms, weak knees, trembling, difficulty breathing or experiencing a sense of unreality. In other words, she feels that she is dealing with something much more serious than anxiety. During an attack she may feel like she is passing out, or in extreme cases, she may think she is having a stroke or heart attack. The symptoms are very frightening.

Because these episodes are so intense and often accompanied by a sense of impending doom, the anxiety sufferer struggles to stay in control. With each panic attack she focuses more and more on the possibility of recurrence, and so begins a pattern of avoidance. For example, if she is anxious at a grocery store, there is a growing fear that an attack might happen at the mall, church, or restaurant.

How can I be supportive of a family member or friend
with an anxiety disorder?

You can help support a family member or friend by lowering your expectations. Lowered expectations allow for any anxiety. Do not, for example, expect him to enter feared situations anxiety-free; do not force him to do things against his will. If he has a difficult time, do not show your disappointment or anger, though these feelings are normal. Above all, do not shame him.

To be supportive, allow for and expect setbacks. If family and friends expect continued, marked improvement, it is difficult for the anxiety sufferer to lower his own expectations. He may do well for a while and handle feared situations almost without anxiety. But suddenly, without warning, his anxiety or panic returns. You can help by reassuring him that setbacks are temporary, normal and a necessary part of recovery.

What do I say?

First, let's look at what *not* to say. The following remarks can be shaming to the person who is trying hard to cope with unexplainable and frightening symptoms. More than likely, she is already hearing this inner dialogue herself.

"What is there to be afraid of?"

"Just pull yourself together!"

"Snap out of it!"

"You mean you're still having this problem?"

"It's all in your head!"

"Is it always going to be this way?"

"Just think positive!"

"Just do it!"

"Don't think about it!"

"I'm really tired of this!"

The following questions and statements are helpful:

"Just take your time."

"If you panic, you panic."

"Try to go with the feeling."

"We can leave whenever you want to."

"You're not crazy."

"It's just a panic attack. Nothing is going to happen to you."

"I'm here if you need me."

"Try to slow down."

"Try not to fight the feeling."

"It takes a lot of courage to do what you're doing!"

"You've been through this before, you'll get through it again."

"You're doing very well!"

"What can I do to help?"

Is the anxiety being used as an excuse?

Every now and then someone at a support group meeting mentions how they have been accused of gaining benefit from their anxiety problem. Their anxiety or panic attacks are seen as an excuse. The truth is that there's little if any benefit from a disorder that disrupts one's life so dramatically, and such accusations only add to the anxiety.

Anxiety sufferers experience much guilt about the fact that their anxiety or panic attacks can put a strain on their relationships with family and friends, especially those closest to them. They are continually afraid of criticism, rejection or abandonment, and want to get well as soon as they can in order to stabilize their relationships and lead "normal" lives again.

How much should I do for him or her?

There is a temptation to help the person with anxiety or panic to the point where she depends on you to take care of everything—grocery shopping, running errands, driving the kids to evening or weekend activities. And she will take all the help you care to give. But she needs to gain the confidence to do these things on her own. It will take time and practice, and you will have to give it all the time it needs. (Putting recovery into a time frame tends to slow down the process.)

As the anxiety or panic sufferer starts to regain some of her independence, she may start to worry that she will be *expected* to perform tasks and go places just as she did before her first attack. But remember: such expectations will only raise her level of anxiety. Just because she was able to drive on the highway or shop at the mall yesterday, doesn't mean she will be able to do so today. The unpredictability of the anxiety or panic is frustrating for the sufferer and family alike. It is important that you try to accept relapses as part of the problem. Let her know that you are there for her on both good days and bad.

I remember accompanying a support group member to take a driver's test. Her phobia had kept her from driving for years. After repeated practice she was now able to take this big step. Keeping her expectations low, she focused on the risk itself and considered "just being there" a tremendous success. Much to her surprise, she passed the test. My surprise came when I realized that I was more excited than she was about passing the test. "Now, I suppose I'll be expected to drive," she said afterward. Anticipating her family's expectations cast a gray cloud over what could have been a celebration of accomplishment.

Because of his panic attacks, my husband is hesitant
  to go places with me

A person who experiences panic attacks needs security; he needs to know that he can leave a feared situation when necessary. He needs to trust that you will turn the car around at any time or leave a social situation at his request without becoming angry or critical. With this trust, he can feel more in control of the situation and will be more likely to take the risk of going places with you. Clearly, this demands a great deal of flexibility on your part and may be frustrating. However, if you express anger or criticism when he is unable to handle certain situations, you will be adding to the anger and criticism he is already directing toward himself and adding to his feeling of failure and shame.

Planning what to do, just in case he needs to leave a feared situation, will help both of you. For him, just knowing there's a way out takes the pressure off of having to do well. Knowing he has the option of leaving a place he fears can actually make it easier for him to remain. Encourage him to take risks, but don't add pressure by forcing him to do things he's not ready for.

If he's not seeing a therapist, suggest that he do so. This problem does not go away by itself. A support group is also useful, since it will give him the opportunity to learn coping strategies and to connect with others who experience the same problem. Some groups encourage support people, like yourself, to attend their meetings to learn more about the disorder and how to deal with it. Be sure to read books and articles on the subject. Watch for seminars or talk shows where it is discussed. You will be amazed at how common anxiety disorders are. The more you know, the less of a mystery your loved one will be and the more relaxed you can be in dealing with the problem. Your acceptance, and a relaxed attitude, will be especially helpful.

It is important for the anxiety sufferer to talk openly about his anxiety. Encourage him to keep talking about his feelings. Ask him how you can help—not with the attitude, *What can I do to fix this so you can be normal again,* but with a sense of *I'm here if you need me.*

Anxiety disorders are treatable. People do recover. But the recovery process takes a lot of time, patience, and courage on the part of the anxiety sufferer *and* the support person. The journey may not be easy, but it can be filled with discovery and growth. It can be rewarding for both of you.

In the following story, Debby talks about ways a support person can be helpful.

Debby's Story

Many of us are involved in a relationship of one kind or another, and we want to explore the many ways that a support person can be helpful, not hindering, in our recovery process. At the same time, we need to understand our significant other's point of view so that both of us can have a better understanding for better communication and more harmony in the relationship. Here are some suggestions:

We need to be able to confide in our support person and tell him our thoughts, no matter how silly or shameful they seem to be. We need to feel safe revealing them, knowing that they will not be laughed at, but accepted as part of our panic disorder.

We need to be able to leave when we choose to leave, instead of staying in a situation we feel we cannot or do not want to handle.

We need our support person to be sensitive about making harmful statements. Critical and judgmental behavior reinforces our own negative self-talk, and thus reinforces our disorder.

Sometimes we need to be alone to renew ourselves and just float through the anxiety. Sometimes we need to be held because we feel like a frightened child.

Points to Remember: *The Support Person*

1. Even without understanding the complexities of anxiety and panic disorders, you can help by showing compassion and a desire to understand what the anxiety sufferer is dealing with.

2. It is important that the anxiety–panic sufferer be able to talk openly about their anxiety and ask for what they need. Let them know that you are there for them on both good days and bad.

3. Do not expect the person who is anxious or panicky to enter feared situations anxiety-free, nor force them to do things against their will.

4. The anxiety–panic sufferer needs the security of knowing they can leave a feared situation when necessary.

5. If they have a difficult time, do not show your disappointment or anger, even though it is normal for you to have these feelings. Above all, do not shame them.

6. Allow for, and expect, setbacks. The anxiety–panic sufferer may do well for a while when, suddenly, their anxiety or panic returns. This unpredictability is frustrating for the sufferer and family alike.

7. Do not accuse them of benefiting from their problem. There's little if any benefit from a disorder that disrupts one's life so dramatically.

8. The anxiety–panic sufferer experiences a great deal of guilt

about the fact that their anxiety problem can put a strain on their relationships with family and friends.

9. It is tempting to help the person until they depend on you for everything. But they need to gain confidence to do things on their own. With time and practice this will happen.

10. Learn what you can about anxiety and panic disorders. Read books and articles on the subject. Watch for seminars and talk shows where the subject is discussed.

BIBLIOGRAPHY & RECOMMENDED READING

Beckfield, Denise. *Master Your Panic and Take Back Your Life!* Atascadero, Calif.: Impact Publishers, 1994.

Bemis, Judith & Amr Barrada. *Embracing the Fear: Learning to Manage Anxiety and Panic Attacks.* Center City: Hazelden, 1994.

Bourne, Edmund J. *The Anxiety & Phobia Workbook.* Oakland: New Harbinger, 1990.

Butler, Kathleen A. *Learning and Teaching Style: In Theory and Practice.* Maynard, MA: Gabriel Systems, Inc., 1984; Gregorc, Anthony F. *An Adult's Guide to Style.* Maynard: Gabriel Systems, Inc., 1982.

Freeman, Lynne. *Panic Free: Eliminate Anxiety/Panic Attacks Without Drugs And Take Control of Your Life.* New York: Barclay House, 1995.

Gardner, James and Arthur H. Bell. *Overcoming Anxiety, Panic, and Depression: New Ways to Regain Your Confidence.* Franklin Lakes, N.J.: The Career Press, Inc., 2000.

Handly, Robert. *Anxiety & Panic Attacks: Their Cause and Cure.* New York: Fawcett, 1987.

Montgomery, Bob and Laurel Morris. *Living With Anxiety: A Clinically Tested Step-by-Step Plan for Drug-Free Management.* Cambridge, Mass.: Perseus Publishing, 2001.

Peurifoy, Reneau Z. *Anxiety, Phobias, & Panic: A Step-by-Step Program for Regaining Control of Your Life.* New York: Warner Books, 1995.

Peurifoy, Reneau Z. *Overcoming Anxiety: From Short-Term Fixes to Long-Term Recovery,* New York: Henry Holt and Company, 1997.

Weekes, Claire. *Hope and Help for Your Nerves.* New York: A Signet Book, 1990.

Weekes, Claire. *Simple, Effective Treatment of Agoraphobia.* New York: Bantam Books, 1976.

Wilson, Reid. *Don't Panic: Taking Control of Anxiety Attacks.* New York: Harper & Row, 1996.

ABOUT THE AUTHOR

Judith Bemis, a recovered agoraphobic, started experiencing panic attacks in 1965. Thinking that it was a serious medical problem, she continually searched for answers concerning the cause, but to no avail. After a period of being semi-housebound, she managed to white-knuckle it until a major setback in 1981 prompted a renewed search for help. A year of cognitive therapy proved to be a turning point in her life.

Wanting to share her freedom with others, she founded Open Door Outreach, Inc., a network of support groups for people with agoraphobia and other related anxiety disorders, and has served as director and facilitator for the organization since 1986. In January of 2007, Open Door merged with NAMI Minnesota (National Alliance on Mental Illness). Ms. Bemis serves on the NAMI Minnesota Board of Directors. She is co-author of *Embracing the Fear, Learning to Manage Anxiety and Panic Attacks* (Hazelden, 1994).

Ms. Bemis holds a Bachelor of Science Degree in Education from the University of Minnesota, and did graduate work at Michigan State University. Before retiring, she taught public school music for thirty-five years and worked as a consultant for two years at Abbot-Northwestern Hospital's Behavioral Medicine Clinic in Minneapolis. She is committed to helping improve the lives of people who suffer with anxiety and panic attacks.

Printed in the United States
150398LV00003B/73/P